YOU BE THE JUDGE 2

A Collection of Ethical Cases and Jewish Answers

Nahum Amsel

ISBN 1-891662-16-3

Copyright © 2002 Nahum Amsel

Published by Torah Aura Productions

TORAH AURA PRODUCTIONS• 4423 FRUITLAND AVENUE, LOS ANGELES, CA 90058
(800) BE-TORAH • (800) 238-6724 • (323) 585-7312 • FAX (323) 585–0327
E-MAIL <MISRAD@TORAHAURA.COM> • VISIT THE TORAH AURA WEBSITE AT WWW.TORAHAURA.COM

MANUFACTURED IN THE UNITED STATES OF AMERICA

Foreword

The "Bet Din" process that has been captured in this book came to life as an accident in a family Torah class I was running at the University of Judaism. It was basically designed to be just a mixer with a little learning attached. It surprised all of us as it quickly became something very powerful.

It started out with circles of families gathered around and serving as juries trying to solve difficult cases. It was fun and interesting to see them try to verbalize their values and their ethics as they struggled to apply them. It was powerful to see the way they grabbed at the pieces of Jewish learning they had at their disposal and twisted them into workable answers. The creativity and the conflict were inspiring.

A few have objected that we have polluted halakhah by letting the unlettered serve as legal decisors (and live with the fantasy that they can make decisions).

A few have objected that the exercise is folly—because religious law no longer has a place in a universe where every opinion is valid.

A few have objected that it was too Reform. Others that it was too Orthodox.

But the truth is, most of the time whether with kids, with families, with seniors—and then again among a broad-based electronic circle in first *Shabbas.Doc* and now *C.Ha*—the Sefat Emet has proved to be right:

> The entire Torah, God's teaching, was given to the Jewish people.
> Each person, however, has a personal Torah,
> a particular life goal that is concealed in the soul.
> When that particular teaching is released to the world
> the person moves toward the truth of his or her being.

Joel Lurie Grishaver

[1] Your Bacon or Your Life?

a well-known Jew-hater with a violent past broke into the rabbi's house and put a gun to his head. The Jew-hater ordered the rabbi to eat a piece of pork (which he had brought with him) or else he would kill the rabbi.

YOU BE THE JUDGE: *Should the rabbi eat the pork to save his life? Also: may he still choose to die rather than eat the pork even if the Torah doesn't demand such a response?*

The Answer to Your Bacon or Your Life

The question is whether a Jew should give up his life rather than eat non-Kosher food at gunpoint.

[a] The Talmud (*Sanhedrin* 74a) says that for 610 of the 613 mitzvot (commandments), a Jew should violate the commandment and the Torah rather than die. This is based on the verse "...AND YOU SHALL LIVE BY (performing) THEM" (Leviticus 18:5), to which the Rabbis of the Talmud (*Yoma* 85b) add "and not die by observing them (the mitzvot)."

[b] The Talmud (*Sanhedrin* 74a) goes on to say that there are three exceptions in which a Jew must give up his or her life rather than commit the sin. These sins are (1) murder, (2) sexual impropriety, and (3) idol worship. Therefore, the answer to our question seems straightforward: the Rabbi must eat the non-Kosher food, rather than give up his life. However, there is an exception. When the entire society is filled with widespread and systematic anti-Semitism, a Jew may not violate even the simplest act or "minor" commandment—even at penalty of death—since this act betrays the Jewish people and desecrates God's name.

The second part of our question, "*May* the Rabbi give up his life rather than eat non-Kosher food" is much more complicated. Although it seems that, based on the Talmud, a person does not have permission to decide what to do in such a case, there exist three different opinions among Jewish authorities.

[a] Maimonides (*Hilkhot Yesodai Torah* 5:1) rules that it is always forbidden to give up one's life in such a circumstance. One who then allows him/herself to be killed rather than eat the non-Kosher food is considered to be the same as a person who committed suicide, which is a sin in Judaism.

[b] Rabbi David ben Zimrah (Egypt, 1479-1573) disagrees and says, "If a person is willing to give up his or her life for Jewish principles, s/he is considered a *tzaddik*—a righteous person. That person is to be praised."

[c] Rabbi Yehuda Rozanes (Turkey, 1658-1727), in his book *Parashat Derakhim*, offers a compromise position. He says that only an established Jewish leader may martyr him/herself when not mandated. However, a lay person or any other Jew is forbidden to accept death rather than violate any of the other 610 mitzvot.

[2] Fake Tzedakah

The Weiss family was watching television one Sunday when a man rang the doorbell. He asked for *tzedakah* (charity) for needy families in Israel who were too poor to afford food and clothing. Mr. Weiss had heard that there was a con artist collecting money around the city. That person pocketed the large sums of money that he received, rather than donating them to those in need. But Mr. Weiss was not sure if this was indeed the "faker" or, rather, a legitimate collector who helped the needy. Mr. Weiss had to make a decision on the spot.

YOU BE THE JUDGE: *Should he give money to this man or not?*

The Answer to Fake Tzedakah

Should we give *tzedakah* to someone who may be a faker?

[a] Certainly, when one is *sure* that the collector is a fake and/or is a wealthy person collecting for him/herself, one is not obligated to give.

[b] However, when one is not certain, an underlying concept of *tzedakah* giving comes into play: as important as it is to give as much as possible, Judaism also considers the feelings of the poor person and the embarrassment factor in how one gives. Refusing to give to a person who is truly in need is extremely embarrassing, and is not permitted.

Maimonides (*Hilkhot Matanot Aniyim* 10:7) lists eight levels of tzedakah giving. As the levels get "higher," the amount of embarrassment felt by the person who needs to ask for help is less and less. The highest of these levels is to help someone to be independent through a job or a loan. This prevents the embarrassment of having to ask for help again in the future. Similarly, Maimonides teaches that it is a higher level to give *less* than a person asks but give it with a pleasant disposition, than to give exactly what the person asks but with a dour face (as this makes the poor person feel bad).

Based on this information, we must conclude that even if nine out of ten people asking for *tzedakah* are fakes, it is preferable in Judaism to give to nine fakes, rather than to refuse them all, and thus embarrass that tenth legitimate poor person.

[c] The Talmud and the Code of Jewish law (*Shulḥan Arukh, Orekh Ḥayyim* 251:10) also say that if a person asks for food, one must give immediately (since the need is immediate) but for clothing (which is not immediate if the person is already clothed), it is permitted to delay.

Therefore, if a person comes to the door and there is a way to verify the situation with an appropriate authority without embarrassing the person, this should be done. If the need is not as immediate as food, it is permitted to take some time to find out whether or not the person is a fake and is dishonestly soliciting money. A homeowner can excuse him/herself for a moment, do some checking into the honesty of the claim, and then make a decision—if it can be done without arousing suspicion and embarrassment.

[3] Freedom of Speech...

Susan told Sharon a really juicy piece of information regarding the personal situation of a mutual friend, Natalie. Susan did not tell Sharon to keep the knowledge a secret, but Sharon knows that Natalie would not want this information spread around.

YOU BE THE JUDGE:

Can Sharon share this information with her best friend Elana?

The Answer to Freedom of Speech...

Should Susan tell this information about Natalie to another friend?

[a] Judaism tells us that one must never reveal *any* information spoken, and that the information must remain a secret until its originator gives specific permission allowing the contents of the conversation to be passed on to others.

[b] The book of Proverbs commands that we "...DO NOT REVEAL THE SECRET OF ANOTHER" (Proverbs 25:9)

[c] The source that teaches that one should never reveal information without permission comes from the Talmud (*Yoma* 4b). Since the Torah always says, "GOD SPOKE TO MOSES *SAYING* (*leymor*)..." and then says "SPEAK TO THE CHILDREN OF ISRAEL..." we have to ask, why all the repetition of "speaking" verbs? The Rabbis teach that the extra "SPEAK TO THE CHILDREN OF ISRAEL" tells us that we must have permission to repeat information that we hear. Otherwise, it is not permitted to pass information along, even when the original bearer did not specifically say, "Don't repeat this."

There are three instances, however, which are exceptions to the rule. In these situations, a person is either permitted or required to repeat information that was given to him or her:

[a] The Talmud (*Arakhin* 16a) says that if the speaker repeats the information in front of three or more people, it is assumed that this information will leak out and, thus, a person may repeat the information without permission.

[b] Based on the verse "AND IF A SOUL SINS...IF HE DOES NOT TESTIFY, THEN HE SHALL BEAR HIS INIQUITY" (Leviticus 5:1), the *Shulhan Arukh* rules (*Rema, Yoreh Deah* 228:33) that if a person is called to testify in a Jewish court, he or she *must* testify and give the pertinent information when asked. This is true *even he or she previously promised not to reveal that information.*

[c] In order to save a person in danger, one *must* break a confidence and reveal a secret (*Shulhan Arukh, Hoshen Mishpat* 426:1).

[4] That's No Job for a Jew...Or Is It?

The Zimmer family was about to hire a maid to clean their rather large house four times a week. Two candidates were interviewed. They were equal in experience and ability, but one was Jewish and the other was not. Mrs. Zimmer did not want to hire the Jewish maid because "this is not the sort of work that Jews should do." Mr. Zimmer felt exactly the opposite: that they should hire that maid, since Jews should help other Jews before non-Jews.

YOU BE THE JUDGE: *Who is right? Should the maid's religion have anything to do with the decision?*

The Answer to That's No Job for a Jew...Or Is It?

The question is whether it is preferable to hire or not to hire a Jewish maid. Many Jewish people feel that it is improper for a Jewish woman to crawl around on the floor doing demeaning work, and to work for another Jew. It disturbs one's Jewish sensibilities. This is how Mrs. Zimmer felt. However, this feeling runs counter to Jewish law and Jewish values.

[a] The idea of involving Jewishness in the choice of whom we hire may seem strange today—but it goes back to a deep notion taught in the Talmud, *"Kol Yisrael Areyvim Zeh-b'Zeh"* (All Jews are interconnected). In other words—Jews are like family to each other. (*Sanhedrin* 27b) The core question here is What is the best way of treating someone who is "like family"?

[b] Maimonides (*Hilkhot Matanot Aniyim* 10:17) states: "The sages commanded that poor and orphans should (serve) a household rather than (non-Jewish) slaves. It is best to use the service of Jews, rather than those from a strange seed, so that (at least) the children of Abraham, Isaac and Jacob should receive benefit and some enjoyment from Jewish property. An increase in (non-Jewish) slaves generates sin. Having Jews work in a household increases mitzvot." The Rambam's statement assumes a time in which everyone kept the ritual and ethical commandments, stopping for afternoon prayers together or paying attention to what things needed to be done to protect the dignity of others. Therefore, giving a Jewish person a job is a basic principle of Judaism, and is preferable to giving the job to a non-Jew.

[c] For a poor person (which we assume to be the socioeconomic category of most maids), providing a job is the highest form of *tzedakah*, and it is preferable to give someone a job rather than a donation (*Shulhan Arukh, Yoreh Deah* 249:6). Rabbi Shabbetai ben Meir, known as *Shach* (Lithuania, 1621-1662) specifically says that each time a Jew employs another Jew, the employer fulfills the mitzvah of tzedakah.

Judaism, therefore, believes that there is no shame in honest labor, no matter what the nature of the job. Although it is a socioeconomic fact of life that recent immigrant groups tend to fill the positions of domestic help, if the chance presents itself, Jews should try to hire other Jews for these positions if all other factors are equal.

[d] One additional issue comes into play here: the issue of protecting all people's dignity. Judaism does not support the idea that non-Jews must play roles that are subservient to Jews. The tradition teaches: Other people's *kavod* (dignity) should be as precious to you as your own. (*Pirke Avot* 2:15)

[5] Which Tzedakah Comes First?

The Levine family was not wealthy, and only had a small amount of money available to them from which to give their portion of *tzedakah*. They knew that there was a poor pious Jew in their neighborhood who could really use the funds. They also knew the local Hillel rabbi who needed money to run Jewish programs on campus for the Jewish students. On top of that, they had a cousin who was also poor and in need.

YOU BE THE JUDGE: *If they only had money to help one of these three needy causes, where should the tzedakah go?*

The Answer to Which Tzedakah Comes First?

The question is who has priority to your *tzedakah*: the local campus Hillel, a poor scholar in the community, or a poor cousin.

[a] Although there is a general obligation to help any Jew in need, based on the verse "YOU SHALL LOVE YOUR NEIGHBOR AS YOURSELF" (Leviticus 19:17), Judaism has a very specific order of priority with regard to *tzedakah* (not only to whom to give, but also how to give). The best method of giving is a loan to a poor person (*Shulḥan Arukh, Yoreh Deah* 249:6). This is based on the verse "IF YOU LEND MONEY TO ANY OF MY PEOPLE WITH YOU WHO IS POOR, YOU SHALL NOT BE A CREDITOR TO HIM, NOR SHALL YOU LAY UPON HIM INTEREST" (Exodus 22:24).

[b] The same Talmudic passage that discusses *how* to give also discusses the order of giving (*Bava Metzia* 71a), and this was later codified into Jewish law (Maimonides, *Hilkhot Matanot Aniyim*, chapter 7 and *Shulḥan Arukh, Yoreh Deah*, chapter 251).

[c] The first priority for *tzedakah* goes to poor relatives living in your home. Money given for children's Torah learning and gifts to parents is included in this category. Within the family itself, the needs of parents who are poor take precedence over those of poor children, who come before poor siblings, and then all other poor relatives. Following one's relatives, the poor of one's own neighborhood take precedence of those from other neighborhoods, followed by the poor of one's town, followed by any poor person in need. The poor of Israel, specifically of Jerusalem, have equal status with those in one's own town. In our days, non-Jewish poor must be given equal consideration along with Jewish poor.

Based on this priority list, the needs of poor people certainly take precedence over other Jewish causes not involving the poor. Hillel's needs, although crucial, take a back seat to helping the needy. And even if a poor scholar of your neighborhood has great financial needs, your poor cousin (because he or she is family) takes priority. It should be noted that according to most commentaries, this priority list is only valid when the financial needs are identical.

[6] Your Money or Her Life...

In a country where kidnapping is fairly common, Mr. Schwartz's wife is kidnapped. The kidnappers demand $2 million in ransom, which is all the money and assets the husband owns. He naturally wants to pay the ransom, but the police and politicians strongly advise him not to pay it. They give him three reasons. First, if the ransom is paid, it will encourage the same group and others to continue kidnapping and demanding ransom. Second, the kidnappers may take his wife again and demand another, higher, ransom, which he may not be able to pay. Third, there is a strong chance that as soon as the first ransom is paid, the wife will immediately be killed, since she may be able to identify the kidnappers. If the ransom is not paid, they argue, the kidnappers will understand kidnapping is not profitable. They also insist that there is a good chance the wife will be returned unharmed. Mr. Schwartz wants to pay the ransom to remove his wife from jeopardy as soon as possible.

YOU BE THE JUDGE: *Should the ransom be paid?*

The Answer to Your Money or Her Life...

Is it right to pay ransom for a kidnapping victim? Might paying "free" the kidnappers to kill the victim, and also encourage future kidnapping?

[a] Based on the verse "YOU SHALL NOT STAND IDLY BY WHEN YOUR FELLOW'S BLOOD IS BEING SPILLED" (Leviticus 19:16), the husband must do everything in his power to save his wife. Even if there is only a very small chance that the wife will be freed after paying that ransom, the husband is obligated to try saving his wife by paying (*Shulḥan Arukh, Orekh Ḥayyim* 329:3). Nonetheless, we still need to ask what to do if paying may hasten her death?

[b] Judaism specifically discusses the mitzvah of paying ransom to free a hostage (apparently this situation was very common in earlier generations). The *Shulḥan Arukh* (*Yoreh Deah* 252:1,3) simply states that *there is no mitzvah more important than this one,* and therefore, it is permitted to take money that had been collected for any other purpose and use it to free a hostage. (Normally rerouting of funds is forbidden unless one asks specific permission from the person who gave the money.) In fact, the *Shulḥan Arukh* continues, anyone who does not perform this Mitzvah is equated to a murderer. However, in the very next line (252:4), there is a confusing line: "One may not redeem a hostage for more than he is worth (a small sum equivalent to payment for physical activity), in order to prevent abuses, so that enemies are not encouraged to continue taking hostages. However, a person is permitted to redeem himself with as much money as he desires."

[c] This Jewish law shows both sides of our issue and Judaism's sensitivity to the conflict. On the one hand, we cannot allow kidnapping to thrive. To try to discourage it, Jewish law says that you may not pay vast sums of money for hostages. On the other hand, a person may do anything to save his or her own life. This tension is also found in the Talmud (*Ketuvot* 52a). It says that if a wife is taken captive, a husband must pay up to ten times her physical value the first time she is kidnapped. Thereafter he may pay ransom only if he wishes to. This is not a passage informing us about the relationship between a husband and wife. Rather, it shows the tension between saving a loved one and discouraging future kidnappers.

Therefore, while the community has an obligation to minimize further kidnapping (and thus not use communal funds to pay exorbitant ransoms), each person can and must do whatever it takes to free him/herself. In addition, there is a specific obligation for family members to pay ransoms and free each other from kidnappers (*Shulhan Arukh, Yoreh Deah* 252: 12). Returning to our specific question, the Jewish answer is now clear. If paying ransom will increase the kidnapped woman's chances of death even slightly, ransom must not be paid. If paying the ransom will increase the chances of the hostage being freed even slightly, then the husband must pay it. Society at large, however, may not pay the ransom for such a hostage, as it will only encourage future kidnappings.

[d] Paying ransom to free a hostage is one of the most praiseworthy commandments. Over the centuries, Jews have lived in places where this has been a necessity. Even though such an act of kindness is required by Jewish Law, one may *not* pay an exorbitant amount if it is demanded by the kidnappers or authorities, even if this means that the hostage will not be freed (*Shulhan Arukh, Yoreh Deah* 252:4). The reason for this ruling is that paying such an exorbitant sum will only encourage future hostage taking, and the community resources will be depleted by paying high ransoms. No individual is worth more than the success of the community.

[7] My Problems or My Community's Problems?

Littletown is having a large problem. Apparently, the sewage from a company that used to be located outside the town's borders (and has since closed its doors), has been leaking into the entire town. Cases of cancer and other diseases have become much more prevalent, and everyone is concerned. Meetings have been called to involve the local and federal governments, and everyone is being asked to put in time to help deal with this issue. Mr. and Mrs. Kayman, however, are both very busy with full time jobs and do not see the need to get involved. They have, in the past, been part of the Temple leadership and the rabbi has specifically asked them to put in their time, effort and ideas for this town problem. When their children ask them to get involved, they explain that their work and personal concerns take precedence over this problem, but the children do not accept their answer.

YOU BE THE JUDGE: *Getting involved is clearly a good thing to do. But, do the Kaymans have an obligation to get involved?*

The Answer to My Problems or My Community's Problems?

The question is whose needs take precedence in Judaism—the private needs of the individual or the needs of the community.

[a] Judaism certainly recognizes the rights and needs of the individual. According to the Midrash (*Bereshit Rabbah* 42:13), the very name "Hebrew" (*ivri*, from the root עבר, meaning "pass over" or "cross the bounds") originally refered to Abraham, because he stood up and challenged his community. Mordekhai, of the story of Purim, is called *Yehudi*—a Jew—according to some interpretations because he was an individualist (*Midrash Esther Rabbah* 4). However, the Jew's role as part of the Jewish community is also a very basic principle in Judaism.

[b] According to the Talmud (*Sanhedrin* 17b), a Jewish scholar may not live in a town unless an organized Jewish community exists. Jews should pray as a community because God cannot reject the prayers of a Jewish community (*Berakhot* 8a). Every Jew, whether he or she wants to be or not, is part of the larger Jewish world community, as it says, "*Kol Yisrael arevim zeh l'zeh*"—"Every Jew is connected to every other Jew"(*Sanhedrin* 27b).

[c] One Talmudic passage shows both the importance of the individual and that of the community. When the Talmud asks why only one human being was originally created, and not many people, several responses are given. One answer is that unlike coins, where each is an exact duplicate of the original mint, God made each person with features merely *similar* to those of the original human being. Each person has different and unique traits. This demonstrates that we are part of the community of human beings (we share similar features and ancestors), but we remain individuals.

[d] When a person is sitting *Shiva* (the first seven days of mourning after losing a loved one, with special mourning rituals that include the community), it is forbidden for that person to learn Torah. Torah learning is considered to be joyous. However, if the community needs this person to teach Torah, he or she is permitted to do so, since the needs of the community override those of the individual (*Shulhan Arukh, Yoreh Deah* 384:1).

Thus, it seems clear that the Kayman children are correct, and their parents should help with the community problems even if they have to sacrifice some of their own needs. The Talmud (*Berakhot* 49b) admonishes anyone who disassociates him/herself from the community, and the Mishnah (*Avot* 2:4) states that one may not abandon the Jewish community "*Al tifrosh min ha-tzibur.*" In fact, the Talmud (*Bava Metzia* 91a) speaks about two actual community leaders mentioned at the beginning of the Book of Ruth, who were expected to help their community's needs during a famine. However, they abdicated their responsibility and moved to the non-Jewish country Moav. Shortly thereafter they died as punishment for their actions. Based on this, Maimonides (*Hilkhot Teshuva* 3:11) states that he who abandons his or her community in time of need, loses his or her entire share in the World to Come, even if no specific sin was committed.

[8] Pay Now—Pray Later?

Israel is once again being threatened by its enemies with a crisis. There is a need for the Jews in North America to mobilize in order to collect funds, organize political pressure in favor of Israel, and even to send volunteers. The rabbi in one city says that a correct response, in addition to these other measures, is to pray, and that a special prayer session should be organized each week to beseech God for help and intervention. While the congregants agree to this concept in principle, they feel that time is of the essence, and this will not really help the practical needs. They simply cannot afford to "waste" the time it will take for these prayers. The rabbi emphatically disagrees and says that time must be taken out for extra prayers, even at the expense of devoting time to other responses.

YOU BE THE JUDGE: *Should they take brakes from fundraising for services? How would you vote?*

The Answer to Pay Now—Pray Later?

The question is: in time of emergency, should Jews take time out in order to pray? In Judaism, prayer is a legitimate avenue to affect change in a person's life or in a nation's history. Therefore, the rabbi is correct in his request, and time must be divided between fund raising, organizing protests and communal prayer.

[a] Before he met his brother Esau, Jacob prepared in three ways for the encounter. He was worried that it would be a bloody, violent confrontation. According to the Midrash (*Pesikta D'Rav Kehana* 19:3) he did three things simultaneously: he prayed, he prepared for war, and he gathered gifts of appeasement. This idea is quoted by Rashi and by Nahmanides in their commentaries on the Torah. It is interesting to note that prayer is *first* on the list.

[b] When the Jewish people were about to fight a battle for Jewish survival in Persia during the Purim story, they fasted and prayed prior to Esther's entering the palace to plead for her people, and prior to fighting the war against Haman's forces of evil. *Tzom Esther*, the Fast of Esther, commemorates our partnership with God in the face of grave danger. We had to pray before going out to defend ourselves.

[c] On Rosh haShanah and Yom Kippur, when Jews plead for their lives, they utter a formula that will save them from an evil decree: "*Teshuvah* (repentance), *tefillah* (prayer), and *tzedakah* (charity) lighten the force of the decree."

[d] The traditional response to help a sick person is to recite psalms as if each were a prayer going up to call God's attentions to our weakened brothers and sisters. In Israel today, religious soldiers, when not actually in battle or training, learn Torah and pray.

[e] The Talmud states that communal prayer, as the Rabbi suggested, has the advantage that it is never completely disregarded by God (*Brakhot* 8a).

[f] But prayer alone is not enough! Rabbi Joseph Albo (Spain, 15th century), in his *Sefer Ikarim,* taught: If God had decreed for a certain farmer a bountiful harvest, but this person is lazy and refuses to seed the soil, the person will be poor that year because of his laziness. Is God responsible for his lack of bountiful harvest? Similarly, a sack of gold is thrown at the feet of a poor person. If he picks it up, all

23

his dreams can be implemented. But if he makes no attempt to pick up the sack, then this man alone is responsible for his lack of good fortune.

[9] Is Stealing the Afikoman Stealing?

There are two types of Passover "*afikoman* games." In many homes, the leader of the Seder hides the *afikoman* and the children search for it. in some seders, however, the leader keeps the precious matzah next two him or her, and the children try to "steal" it without being noticed.

As Shira and David, the Weinstein children, grew older, they began to question the practice each Pesa<u>h</u> of "stealing" the *afikoman*. While they enjoyed the presents, they also took very seriously the concepts that their parents and Hebrew School teachers had taught them about honesty. How could it be that Judaism advocates stealing the *afikoman*, even if it is only a game? They proposed to abolish this time-honored Pesa<u>h</u> custom when they went to their cousin's Seder, where there would be small children. The adults did not want to throw out the old custom.

YOU BE THE JUDGE: *Who is right: Shira and David or the adults?*

The Answer to Is Stealing the Afikoman Stealing?

The question is, how can we permit "stealing" the *afikoman*, thereby teaching children that it is permissible to steal?

[a] Some opinions (*M'orai Ohr*, for instance) say that it is praiseworthy to desist from this custom precisely for the objection raised.

Most disagree and find that "stealing" the *afikoman* is all right. Take a look:

[b] The Talmud (*Pesaḥim* 109a) gives us the overriding reason why this custom is encouraged: in order to keep the children awake. Since being at the seder and telling the Passover story is the only mitzvah in the Torah in which children (minors, not at the age of bar or bat mitzvah) must participate (Exodus 13:8), it is crucial that the children remain awake as long as possible. The most effective method of accomplishing this is by playing the "game" of taking the *afikoman*, later to be traded in for valuable prizes.

[c] No child falls asleep from boredom as long as the *afikoman* ransom has not been arranged. Maimonides (*Hilkhot Ḥametz u-Matzah* 7:3) codifies this practice by stating that "the matzah is grabbed from one another."

But although we understand the underlying reason for this practice, the Weinstein children seem to have a point, and the question remains: how can Judaism condone such a practice? We know that in Judaism the ends never justify the means. What, then, is the deeper meaning of this custom, and what is its legitimacy?

[d] Rabbi Pinḥas HaLevi Horowitz (Germany, 1730-1805) suggested a novel and interesting approach: We know that God promised Abraham that the Jews would leave Egypt with great wealth (Genesis 15:14). This is repeated in the Torah when God commands the people to ask the Egyptians for gold and silver (Exodus 3:21-22). But when did this "asking" take place? If it had happened before the great plague of the First Born, on the night of the seder, then the Egyptians would not have been too keen on giving their valuable possessions. It could not have happened the next morning, as everyone was rushed to leave Egypt. There was not even time for the bread to bake properly, and that is why we have matzah. So, the taking of the Egyptian riches must have occurred *during* the night of the seder, when only the children were allowed out of the house. God had specifically commanded that "NO PERSON MAY GO OUT OF HIS DOOR UNTIL THE MORNING" (Exodus 12:22). During that night, the adults could not go out, *but the children could.* It was, therefore, the children who took the gold and silver of Egypt, fulfilling God's promise. Thus, the practice today may be considered a reenactment of what occurred in Egypt on that fateful night.

And lest anyone believe that this is actually stealing, the Talmud (*Sanhedrin* 91a) discusses this question. Alexander the Great asked about this "borrowed" Egyptian gold and silver that was never returned. The people answered that when they were paid the wages of 210 years of slave labor (many more times the amount of the gold and silver), they would gladly give back the riches. Thus, it was not stealing at all, but rather a meager payment for their work. Nehama Leibwoitz (*Studies in Shemot, Parashat Bo*) explains that the Torah expression (*lishol mai-im*) does not connote the act of borrowing, but, rather, receiving a gift (from the Egyptian people) that is not intended to be returned. Therefore, it was not stealing at all.

[10] Run from His Life

Mr. Polsky was walking along on the street and saw a friend of his being mugged. He knew of a Jewish law that states that one must save someone who is in danger. But he thought that by trying to save this person's life, he might be putting his own life in danger.

YOU BE THE JUDGE: *What should he do?*

The Answer to Run from His Life

The questions are: should a person help a friend who is being attacked? And does the potential danger outweigh the duty, if there is one, to help that friend?

[a] It certainly is a mitzvah to save a person in danger of dying, as it says, "YOU SHALL NOT STAND BY THE BLOOD OF YOUR NEIGHBOR" (Leviticus 19:16 and *Sanhedrin* 73a).

[b] But there is also a mitzvah to preserve one's own life, as it says "AND YOU SHALL LIVE BY THEM (THE COMMANDMENTS)" (Leviticus 18:5) The Talmud expands on this and explains "You shall live by them (the mitzvot) and not die by them (*Sanhedrin* 74a). Therefore, one may not sacrifice one's life to save someone else.

The real dilemma comes into play, then, when there is definite danger to someone else and only possible danger to you. Is the obligation to save the person or to keep yourself out of harm's way?

[c] The proofs from the stories in the Bible are inconclusive. On the one hand, in the Book of Exodus, the midwives put themselves in possible danger to save Jewish babies in definite danger (Exodus 1:16-17) when Pharaoh decrees that Jewish babies should be killed. Similarly, Esther puts herself in possible danger to save the Jewish people from definite danger (*Esther* 4:8-5:1).

[d] On the other hand, God specifically tells Moses to wait until he is out of danger before returning to Egypt to save the Jewish people, who are in definite danger: "GOD SAID TO MOSES, 'GO, RETURN TO EGYPT, ALL THE PEOPLE WHO DEMAND YOUR LIFE HAVE DIED'" (Exodus 4:19).

[e] The *Hagahot Maymaniyot*, quoted by the *Beit Yosef* commentary on the *Tur*, a Jewish Law code (*Hoshen Mishpat* 426) quotes the Jerusalem Talmud which says that in every case a person must try to save a person in danger because his danger is only a possibility while the danger of the person in distress is definite.

[f] However, the *Beit Yosef* is also the author of the Code of Jewish Law, the *Shulhan Arukh*, and *never codifies this statement as a law which must be followed*. Thus, he rejects this opinion, as does *Mishneh*

Berurah (*Orekh Hayyim* 329:28:19), and says that one may not put him/herself in possible danger to save someone in definite danger.

[g] Based on the above, Rabbi David Ben Zimrah (Egypt, 16th century) concludes that if there is definite danger, one may not even try to save someone. If it is possible danger, one may try if one wishes, but is not obligated. If there is no danger, then one is obligated to save a person in danger.

Our only problem now is defining definite, possible, and no danger. Even if a lifeguard is fully trained and experienced, there always is *some* danger in trying to save a drowning person. Does this *halakhah* imply that the lifeguard should never try to save someone? It has been concluded that if the odds of putting oneself in danger are 1 in 10, then this is called definite danger, and one may not even attempt the rescue. If the odds are 1 in 100, then this is considered possible danger and one *may* try to save the person, but need not do so. Less than 1 in 1000 odds, are not even called possible danger, and one would be obligated to save a person in danger.

[11] Room Service...and Then Some

The Epsteins have spent part of their vacation staying at a posh hotel. As the great vacation draws to a close, members of the family decide that they want souvenirs from their terrific vacation. Fifteen-year-old Jonathan decides to pack a hotel towel, with the hotel's logo, into his suitcase. His mother decides to bring home the unused bottles of hotel shampoo that are in the bathroom, and eight-year-old Esther takes the stationery and pens from the desk in their room.

YOU BE THE JUDGE: *Mr. Epstein is incensed and claims that all these acts are outright stealing. Jonathan and the others argue that the cost of these momentos are already included in the exorbitant hotel price, and, besides, everyone does it. The father is insistent that these items are not included in the cost of the room, and it is indeed stealing. Who is right?*

The Answer to Room Service...and Then Some

Is it considered stealing to take objects from a hotel room? In order to answer this question, we must first define the act of stealing. What is it? Most people will simply answer "taking something that does not belong to you." But this cannot be a complete definition. If a child takes food from the refrigerator in his or her home (without asking the parents), based on this definition, we can say that this is stealing, since the food does not "belong" to the child. And lest someone argue that anything which the parents own automatically also belongs to the children, then it should be permitted for children to take $100 from their parents wallet without asking. And, yet, almost everyone agrees that taking this money *is* stealing. What, then, is the difference between taking food from a refrigerator (not stealing) and taking money from a parent's wallet (stealing)?

It is clear that the parents *do not mind* if a child takes food from the fridge, but they *do mind* when the same child takes money from their wallets. Thus, our definition of stealing must be amended to read, "Taking something that does not belong to you, *if the owner minds.*"

[a] The concept of *ye-ush*, giving up on having the stolen item returned, or "minding" if it is taken, is the basis of determining if an object is stolen or not according to the Talmud (*Sukkah* 30a). If a person is not sure whether the owner would mind (have *ye-ush*) if something were taken, then the Talmud would disallow taking the items.

[b] Consider what a group of people doing the same thing can do to your sense of morality: "Ten people join together to steal a beam, and are not ashamed in each other's presence" (*Kiddushin* 80b). Does the fact that everyone in the family except the father is involved make a difference?

Now let's get into our case, item by item, since we have now determined that, according to Jewish Law, *ye-ush* is our test for whether or not something is considered stolen or not. Before you read our opinions, determine for yourselves: would the hotel management 'mind' if you took a towel? the shampoo? the pen and stationary?

Clearly, most hotels "mind" very much when guests take home the hotel's towels. In fact, many hotels SELL their towels in the gift shop. Thus, taking hotel towels is indeed stealing (unless the owner or manager gives specific permission to take the towels).

What about the unused shampoo? Would the hotel "mind" if that is taken? Numerous surveys show that most hotel managements do not mind if the shampoo is taken, since this is included in the cost of the room. Therefore, taking shampoo is not stealing.

What about the pens and stationary? Here, it is even clearer that the hotel gives away these objects, since they serve to advertise the hotel. Some hotels even post a sign that the pens and stationery are complimentary. Clearly, no hotel "minds" when these items are taken. Therefore, Mr. Epstein is wrong to accuse everyone of stealing. Jonathan is indeed stealing the hotel towels, but Mrs. Espstein and Esther are not stealing in taking the shampoo and stationery.

[12] If He Willed it, Is it a Dream?

Jeremy Stein had a dream in which his father, who had died two years earlier, appeared to him. In the dream, his father told him that he had hidden $10,234 under a floorboard in the attic before his death. He specified which particular floorboard, and then told his son that the money was owed to their synagogue. He had pledged it, but had never actually given the money to the shul. When Jeremy awoke, he immediately checked that particular floorboard in the attic and, amazingly, discovered precisely $10,234.

YOU BE THE JUDGE: *Must Jeremy now give the money to the synagogue as his father specified, or not?*

The Answer to If He Willed it, Is it a Dream?

How do we view dreams? Should we act upon the information conveyed in dreams or not?

[a] The Torah records numerous people who dreamed significant dreams. God usually appeared to prophets in dreams. Even non-Jews such as Avimelech (Genesis 20:6-7) and Bilaam (Numbers 22:9-13) had significant dreams in which God appeared to them. Therefore, it seems that dreams are important in Judaism and should be taken seriously. In fact, the entire history of the Jewish people was impacted by the dreams that Joseph had, which caused the brothers to hate him and get rid of him. By interpreting the dreams of Pharaoh's butler, and those of Pharaoh himself, Joseph was able to rise quickly to power and save his starving brothers by providing them with food. Joseph thus sustained the Jewish people and brought them to Egypt to grow into a nation. Dreams in the Torah certainly are important. But what about the everyday dreams of everyday people like Jeremy Stein?

[b] The Talmud (*Brakhot* 55b) expresses two opposite ideas about dreams. On one hand it quotes one source which says that today's dreams have absolutely no significance (*Zechariah* 40:2). On the other hand they quote another source showing that dreams indeed have significance (Numbers 12:6). Shmuel resolves the contradiction by stating that *some* dreams today have significance while others do not. The problem is that it is not clear how to determine which dreams are the significant ones.

[c] Rabbi Baḥiya, who lived hundreds of years before Sigmund Freud, attempted to quantify which dreams are the significant ones. He explains (commentary to Genesis 41:1) that there are three causes for dreams: 1) food that was eaten during the day 2) thoughts a person had during the day 3) dreams caused by a person's spirit or soul. The first two are insignificant, while the third has significance.

[d] Another Talmudic passage (*Sanhedrin* 30a) records an almost duplicate case to Jeremy Stein's dream, in which a person dreamed that his father appeared and told him where money was hidden. He then instructed his son to return the money to the Temple. In that case, the Talmud rules that the man *need not* return the money and may keep it, even if he finds the exact amount of money in the precise place that his father had told him in the dream. The *Shulḥan Arukh* (*Ḥoshen Mishpat* 255:9) codifies this into Jewish law. Thus, Jeremy may indeed keep the money.

[e] However, the same Law Code codifies another law about a man who dreams about taking an oath. When he wakes up, the Law Code says, he *should* nullify the oath he had made in the dream (*Shulḥan Arukh, Yoreh Deah* 210:2). This proves that dreams have significance. How can we reconcile these two rulings?

[f] Numerous commentaries have attempted to explain both of these rulings. The *Teshbetz* Responsa (Sections II, #128) explains that since we cannot know which dreams are truly significant, we operate in Jewish law from a standpoint of doubt. We do not transfer money out of doubt (hence Jeremy can keep the money), but we do nullify a possible oath (which is a sin, *issur*) out of doubt.

[13] Should Bernie Stand on his Head?

bernie Schwartz has always been careful to honor his father and grant his requests, both as good Jew and as a good son. But recently, Bernie father was diagnosed with Alzheimer's disease and began requesting absurd things from his son. One day he asked Bernie to stand on his head for twenty minutes. The next day he asked him to paint his den, even though it had been painted less than six months earlier.

YOU BE THE JUDGE: *Should Bernie listen to his father and fulfill these strange requests? Why or why not?*

The Answer to Should Bernie Stand on his Head?

As Jews, we want to honor the Torah's commandments at all times. Yet, there are outside and unexpected influences that make us reevaluate exactly how to perform mitzvot. Consider the following about our case:

[a] Even for perfectly healthy parents, the Midrash (*Tanhuma, Eikev* 2) says that the mitzvah to honor one's parents is called the "most difficult commandment in the Torah" to fulfill, and is a mitzvah that is even more important than honoring God (Jerusalem Talmud, *Peah* 3b). Technically, the mitzvah regarding parents involves *kavod* (honor), i.e., keeping a parent's dignity by feeding, clothing and helping him or her exit and enter; and *yirah* (awe), which involves the acts of not sitting or standing in a parent's place, not contradicting, and not siding publicly against a parent who is in an argument (*Kiddushin* 31b). However, most authorities agree that a child is obligated to honor any reasonable request by a parent (Midrash *Yalkut Shimoni, Mishle* 23 and *Shulḥan Arukh, Yoreh Deah* 240:8).

[b] When does a request by a parent become unreasonable? The Talmud (*Kiddushin* 31a) cites the case of Rabbi Assi. His mother was senile, and first she requested that her son bring her jewels, which he did. Then, she requested that he find her a husband, which he tried to do. But when his mother insisted that Rabbi Assi find her a husband as young and handsome as he was (a very unreasonable request), Rabbi Assi left the house and moved to Israel. Thus, we see that even this rabbi did not comply with such an unreasonable request. Maimonides (*Hilkhot Mamrim* 6:10) codifies this idea, and later authorities (*Shiurim Mitzuyanim Ba-Halakhah* 143:4, 10) support the view that irrational requests by parents may be ignored. Therefore, Bernie Schwartz is not obligated to carry out the absurd requests of his father (although he may do so if he wishes).

[c] It should be noted that if a parent asks a child to violate any Torah law, it is forbidden for the child to comply with the request (Maimonides, *Hilkhot Mamrim* 6:12).

Just as important, however, is the *manner* in which a child does or does not listen to a parent. A child must always maintain a parent's dignity and respect at all times (whether complying or not), even if the parent is no longer competent or fully functioning mentally (*Shulḥan Arukh, Yoreh Deah* 242:8,13). The reason is explained in the Talmud (*Berakhot* 8b): A person who is senile is compared to a Holy Ark that is now empty (of a Torah). Even though the ark no longer contains holiness, it still must be accorded respect because it once did contain holiness. So, too, a person who no longer has a fully functioning mind must be accorded respect for what he or she possessed in the past. Similarly, the Talmud continues, it is for this reason that the shattered first set of the tablets of the Ten Commandments were placed in the original Holy Ark along with the second set of tablets. This demonstrates that something which once had value, but no longer has intrinsic value, must still be accorded respect according to its previous holiness or value.

[14] Bar Mitzvah Blues...

fifteen-year-old David had been caught shoplifting. When David's parents' friends mentioned to them that they had to take some responsibility for David's actions, they retorted that as Jews, their responsibility ended with David when he became a bar mitzvah (Son of the Commandments. At the age of 13, boys in the Jewish tradition become legally responsible for mitzvot (commandments) and for civil matters). Although general society still recognizes a fifteen-year-old as a minor, Judaism says that David is legally responsible and is independent at the age of thirteen. Being good Jews, the parents say that they no longer are responsible for David. The father even recalls reciting the blessing absolving himself of David's future sins.

YOU BE THE JUDGE: *Are David's parents correct? Are they absolved from any responsibility for David's actions after Bar Mitzvah? Or are they still responsible Jewishly nevertheless?*

The Answer to Bar Mitzvah Blues...

Is a parent responsible for the actions of a post-bar/bat mitzvah child?

[a] From a Jewish perspective, does a parent bear some responsibility for a post-bat or bar mitzvah teenager? It is certainly true that a child over the age of thirteen is recognized as an adult in Jewish law, and is responsible for his or her actions. This teen now bears the responsibility and consequences for his or her judgments that lead to his or her actions. This is made public when a parent recites the blessing at the bar or bat mitzvah ceremony: "Blessed be the Eternal... Who exonerates me from the sins of this one (child)." However, we will see that although the child is responsible, the relationship between a parent and child (and thus the parent's responsibility for the child) is not severed at when a child becomes a bat or bar mitzvah.

[b] Even after becoming a bar or bat mitzvah, the mitzvah to honor (and listen to) one's parents continues throughout one's life. In addition, if a child continues to live in a parent's home (the situation with most teenagers today), Jewish law continues to attach a legal responsibility by a parent for a child. For example, a lost object found by such a child belongs to the parent and not the teen. That act of a child living in the parents' home gives the parents some responsibility. (Talmud, *Bava Metziah* 12b and *Shulhan Arukh, Hoshen Mishpat* 270:2).

[c] The Talmud (*Kiddushin* 30a) also brings an argument about the optimum age at which a parent has maximum effect upon a child. One opinion is that this takes place between the ages of 16-22, while the other opinion holds that it is between 18-24 years old. This clearly shows a belief that parents continue to have great influence upon post bar and bat mitzvah children. In fact, according to Rashi's commentary on that passage, a parent's impact at these ages is even greater than before.

[d] In yet another passage (*Shabbat* 54b), Judaism holds an adult responsible for all the sins that he or she could have prevented in his or her household but did not prevent. Therefore, although David must certainly take responsibility for his act of shoplifting, his parents also continue to bear some responsibility as long as the teen lives in their home.

[15] Do You Believe in Miracles?

At the Seder table, after discussing the miracles of the Exodus, the Weiss family began talking about modern times. Mrs. Weiss said that there are no miracles today, but her son, Jonathan, said that miracles still exist. As an example, he used the Six-Day War in 1967, in which Israel defeated seven Arab nations in six days. His older sister Sharon said it was a miracle when 39 scuds hit Israel during the Gulf War, and only one person died, and even the creation of the state of Israel itself was miraculous. Mr. Weiss could not make up his mind whether these events are indeed considered miraculous, as his children believe, or whether miracles do not exist today at all, as his wife believes.

YOU BE THE JUDGE: *Who is right?*

The Answer to Do You Believe in Miracles?

Do miracles exist today?

[a] If, by definition, a miracle is a supernatural event (one which defies the laws of nature), then this type of miracle indeed no longer exists. The reasons given are: a) people today would not accept these events as miraculous from God due to a lower spiritual level (*Berakhot* 20a) and b) there is no longer a Temple in Jerusalem, where many supernatural miracles occurred on a daily basis. Soon after the Jews' dispersion into the Diaspora, which followed the destruction of the first Temple (70 CE), a major event in Jewish history occurred, which shows us how the nature of miracles changed forever:

[b] The Purim story (the story of Mordechai and Esther, which occurred during that time period) was a series of events that certainly were not supernatural. And yet, these events, which seem political and coincidental in nature, are called miracles. The prayer recited by Jews to celebrate Purim is called *Al Ha-Nisim* ("For the miracles"). Therefore, even though the events of the Purim story do not seem particularly miraculous, or even seem to be from God, they are labeled as miracles. They seem less miraculous even than the Scud missiles of the Gulf War that failed to kill Israelis. This non-supernatural type became the form of miracles from that point onward in history. This is also one reason that God's name is not mentioned in the Book of Esther, making it the only book of the Bible not to contain direct references to God. This demonstrates that although God was certainly there and was involved in the miracle of Purim, God's role was not obvious (as it is in supernatural miracles). Based on this, Jonathan Weiss is correct that all of these modern events in Jewish history would be considered miraculous. They are natural miracles like the story of Purim.

[c] There is a third type of miracle in Judaism as well. These are everyday events that occur thousands of times. If any of these events (such as a person taking a single step) were to occur only once, everyone would agree that it is a miracle. For example, if there were only one baby's birth or one sunset each year, then everything and everyone would stop to witness these great miracles. Judaism believes that the fact that these occur daily makes them no less miraculous. We thank God in the *Modim* prayer of the *Amidah* for "your miracles that are with us each day."

It is interesting that in Judaism, of the three types of miracles mentioned, the supernatural is considered the *least* miraculous. More miraculous is the natural miracle, while the everyday miracle is the most miraculous of all (see *Nedarim* 41a, *Pesaḥim* 118a).

[16] Knowing Who Shall Live and Who Shall Die?

Susie's good friend Jane accidentally finds out a secret about Susie's fiancé Judah: he has a debilitating medical condition, which will result in his death within two years. Judah has not told Susie, his bride-to-be, about his condition.

YOU BE THE JUDGE: *Should Jane tell her or not?*

The Answer to Knowing Who Shall Live and Who Shall Die?

Should a person reveal important, confidential information to a friend about her if the fiancé himself did not reveal it?

[a] In general, a Jew may not reveal information that is told to him or her, even if the provider of the information did not request that it be kept secret (*Yoma* 4b). However, if the information will potentially save a life, then a person is obligated to reveal such information, even if sworn to secrecy (*Shulḥan Arukh, Ḥoshen Mishpat* 426:1). The values of trust and saving a life have to be weighed carefully here.

[b] In the situation presented, which deeply affects the lives of the people involved, the Chofetz Chaim (*Shemirat Ha-Lashon*, 9:2, example 3, paragraph 7) states that the laws against speaking *lashon ha-ra* (evil talebearing) do not apply. Therefore, Jane *should* tell Susie about Judah's debilitating condition, but only if four conditions are present: 1) the danger to the person (Judah) must be real and imminent. If Judah's disease would cause his death only thirty years later, then the information may not be revealed; 2) One may not exaggerate the information while disclosing it. Thus, Jane cannot say that the disease will kill Judah within six months; 3) The motive for revealing the information must be pure, i.e. only to help the receiver of the information. It may not be undertaken for personal gain or for revenge against a person one dislikes; and, 4) The information must greatly affect the relationship. If the friend knows in advance that the couple is so much in love that they will surely still marry anyway, it is forbidden to reveal such information.

It should be noted that if the person can accomplish the same goal, i.e., breaking the engagement, without having to break a confidence, then one may not reveal such information in that case.

[17] Will the Cat Come Back?

Ruthie is passing by a street when a cat with a collar on (indicating it has an owner) follows her. She wants to pick it up and return it to its owner, but immediately realizes that it will take a lot of time, effort and money to give back this cat. After all, in addition to the time it will take to care for her, Ruthie will have to feed her and pay for ads to let people know where the cat is.

YOU BE THE JUDGE: *What is the right thing to do here? Should she pick it up and try to return it or not?*

The Answer to Will the Cat Come Back?

The question is about the obligation to return lost objects found on the street which would occupy much time and some expense.

[a] In most societies, no one expects or requires anyone to pick up such an object. If one does so it is viewed as so extraordinary that the returner expects a reward. In Judaism, though, the returning of a lost object is mandatory, and a person is *guilty of a sin* if he or she merely passes by a lost object without retrieving it. The Torah emphasizes this when it says "YOU SHALL NOT WATCH YOUR NEIGHBOR'S OX OR HIS SHEEP GO ASTRAY, AND HIDE YOURSELF FROM THEM; YOU SHALL IN ANY CASE BRING THEM AGAIN TO YOUR NEIGHBOR. AND IF YOUR NEIGHBOR IS NOT NEAR YOU, OR IF YOU DO NOT KNOW YOUR NEIGHBOR, THEN YOU SHALL BRING IT TO YOUR OWN HOUSE, AND IT SHALL BE WITH YOU UNTIL YOUR NEIGHBOR SEEKS AFTER IT, AND YOU SHALL RETURN IT. IN LIKE MANNER SHALL YOU DO WITH A DONKEY; AND SO SHALL YOU DO WITH A GARMENT; AND WITH EVERY LOST THING OF YOUR NEIGHBOR'S, WHICH THAT HAS BEEN LOST AND YOU HAVE FOUND; YOU MAY NOT HIDE YOURSELF FROM THIS RESPONSIBILITY." (Deuteronomy 22:1-3).

Since the verse specifically speaks about the return of lost animals, Ruthie would have to return the cat, especially since the collar is an identifying sign for the owner. If there is no identifying sign, including the location in which the animal is found, then the finder can keep it since we assume the owner gave up all hope of retrieving such an object or animal. (*Shulhan Arukh, Hoshen Mishpat* 259:2).

[b] What about Ruthie's expenses? Of course the finder can later charge the owner for expenses such as feeding the animal (*Shulhan Arukh, Hoshen Mishpat* 267:22). Similarly, should Ruthie need to take off time from work to find the owner, these expenses can also be recovered (*Shulhan Arukh, Hoshen Mishpat* 265:1). If the expenses become greater than the worth of the object, then (and only then) would the finder not be obligated to retain the object and try to return it.

48

[18] The Talk Show that Goes Boom

A talk show host intentionally brings two groups onto his show in order to incite them. One is a neo-Nazi fringe group and the other is a militant black group. A fight naturally breaks out, and numerous people get injured. They sue the talk show host for inciting this "riot." At the Shabbat table, the Becker family discusses whether the host can be found guilty from a Jewish perspective. On the one hand, Judaism believes in free will, and each person is therefore a "free agent" to commit or not to commit any act. Based on this argument, the talk show host is not guilty. On the other hand, he intentionally brought these groups together to incite them to fight and improve ratings.

YOU BE THE JUDGE: *Is the talk show host guilty from a Jewish perspective?*

49

The Answer to The Talk Show that Goes Boom

Who is responsible for violence that breaks out?

[a] It is true that from a Jewish perspective each person above the age of bar or bat mitzvah is responsible for his or her actions. Maimonides teaches (*Hilkhot Kelayim* 10:31) about a person who dresses another person with clothing that violates Jewish Law. (Torah forbids Jews from wearing any fabric that mixs wool and linen.) If the person being dressed is unaware of the nature of the clothes, then the "clother" is guilty of the sin. However, if the person being clothed *was* aware of the sinful clothing and did nothing to stop it, then he or she is indeed guilty. Therefore, the rioters must indeed be responsible for their actions as well as any damage they caused. They knew that violence was wrong. But this does not necessarily exonerate the inciter (i.e. the "clother") from being guilty as well. Is the person who incited the sin also guilty?

[b] One of the commandments in the Torah is "YOU SHALL NOT PLACE A STUMBLING BLOCK BEFORE A BLIND" (*Al Ti'ten Mikhshol Lifnei ha-Iver*) (Leviticus 19:14). All of the commentaries understand that this verse refers to more than an actual blind person or an actual stumbling block. It is expanded to refer to any person who knowingly causes another person to "stumble" in any act or into any sin, while the sinner is "blind" to the sin as it is being committed.

[c] The Talmud (*Avoda Zara* 6b) refers to a case of a Nazirite who has taken an oath not to drink wine. If you offer him wine, and he drinks it, then you have violated the prohibition against placing a stumbling block before the blind. Here, the Nazirite certainly is aware of the sin, but is "blinded" by his desire to drink wine, which you facilitate.

[d] The precedent for determining guilt for both the inciter and the actual sinner can be found in the very first sin in the Torah. The serpent was severely punished for inciting the woman to violate God's word by eating the fruit. Soon after, we learn that Eve's claim "I was just following orders" (Genesis 3:13-16) was not a legitimate defense and Eve was also punished. So, too, the rioters may not claim that it is not their fault since they were goaded to sin.

[19] Wedding the Appetite

Mr. Kamen was the vice president of his synagogue, in charge of collecting *tzedakah* for community members in financial need. One popular member, Mr. Kahn, was about to pay for his daughter's wedding, but, unbeknownst to his friends, he had just fallen on hard financial times. Mr. Kahn secretly appealed to Mr. Kamen for help in making a modest wedding, and Mr. Kamen agreed to make an appeal without mentioning names. When Mrs. Kamen overheard this, she begged her husband to publicly mention Mr. Kahn's name in the appeal. A general appeal to the congregation for *hakhnassat kallah*- helping a bride get married, would only garner small donations. However, Mr. Kahn's popularity would bring in at least five times the amount.

YOU BE THE JUDGE: *Should Mr. Kamen keep the appeal secret and receive less money or announce the recipient and receive a much greater amount?*

The Answer to Wedding the Appetite

Should the cause of a *tzedakah* drive be made public, or should the recipients and purpose of the money remain a secret?

[a] The mitzvah of *tzedakah* is great indeed. It is written that this mitzvah has the ability to grant life and death (Proverbs 10:2). Maimonides calls it the most important positive mitzvah in the Torah (*Hilkhot Matanot Aniyim* 10:1). However, the importance of preserving a person's dignity in the process of giving is paramount. That is why the concept of the *pushke* (*tzedakah* box) was developed—so that neither the giver nor the receiver would know the identity of the other, thus preserving the dignity of the receiver. Therefore, Maimonides states that it is preferable to give *less tzedakah* than requested, but with a smile, than to give what is asked for by the poor person but with dour face (*Hilkhot Matanot Aniyim* 10:13-14).

[b] Although it is true that Mr. Kahn would receive far greater donations if his name were announced, he would suffer more shame. His friends would now know of his financial plight. That indignity is far worse than receiving less money. Therefore, Mr. Kamen should not listen to his wife, and should omit Mr. Kahn's name from his appeal.

[20] When Cheaters Prosper

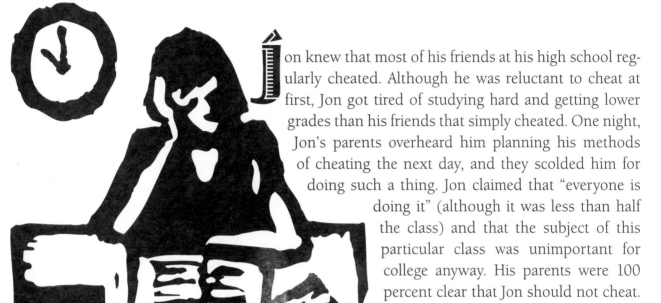

Jon knew that most of his friends at his high school regularly cheated. Although he was reluctant to cheat at first, Jon got tired of studying hard and getting lower grades than his friends that simply cheated. One night, Jon's parents overheard him planning his methods of cheating the next day, and they scolded him for doing such a thing. Jon claimed that "everyone is doing it" (although it was less than half the class) and that the subject of this particular class was unimportant for college anyway. His parents were 100 percent clear that Jon should not cheat. Jon said that many adults regularly cheat by exceeding the speed limit, cheating on income taxes, or doing personal business at work. Why should he suffer and be different?

YOU BE THE JUDGE: *Is Jon's argument good enough? Should his parents let him cheat?*

The Answer to When Cheaters Prosper

The question is whether there is any legitimacy to cheating, especially if the material is not "important." From a Jewish perspective, the relevancy of the information does not matter. The "Jewish" reasons that one may not cheat on exams come from the understanding of the Hebrew expression for cheating, *genaivat da'at* (stealing of thoughts).

[a] Cheating is a form of stealing in Judaism. What is being stolen, and from whom? The concept of *genaivat da'at* is understood to be the obtainment of undeserved good will. As a result of cheating on one or more tests, Jon's teacher will think that he is a better student than he really is. The teacher will also believe that Jon mastered the material taught. This is what is forbidden. And this kind of stealing is worse than any other kind of stealing, including robbing a bank, according to the *Tosefta* (*Bava Kamma* 7: 3).

[b] In addition to "stealing" from his teachers, Jon is also stealing from his parents, who have paid great sums of money so that Jon will receive a complete education and learn all the material. He is fooling them as well. Over the long haul, Jon is also "stealing" from the college which will accept him based, in part, on his grades, which are now inflated and not properly earned. He is also "stealing" from the student (with a slightly lower GPA than Jon's) who will be denied admission to that college, and whose place in the university Jon will take. Finally, Jon is "stealing" from himself, because, by continuing this process, he may eventually come to believe that the only way to achieve excellence is through illegality. In reality, Jon is capable of achieving this effect through his abilities and effort.

[c] While it may be true that others in society do things that are improper or immoral, there can be no justification based on what others are doing. Judaism recognizes that peer pressure is a powerful force in life (Maimonides, *Hilkhot Deot* 6:1), but each person is given free choice (Deuteronomy 30:15,19) and thus retains the ultimate responsibility for his or her choices. Cheating anyone, Jew or non-Jew, is clearly a violation of the Torah (Maimonides, *Hilkhot Mehira* 18:1), and even cheating on one test or quiz is a violation of the Torah's concept of stealing (Maimonides, *Hilkhot Genaiva* 1:2).

[21] Cops and Robbers

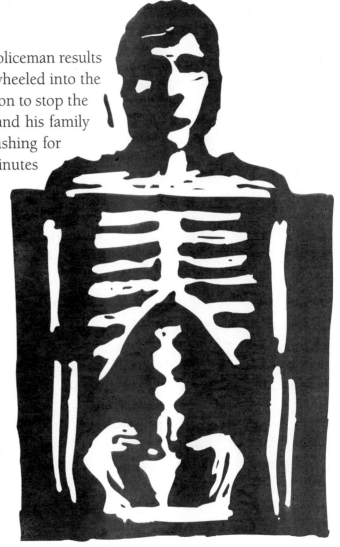

a shoot-out between a mugger and a policeman results in the officer being wounded. He is wheeled into the ER (Emergency Room), and needs an operation to stop the internal bleeding. His fellow police officers and his family are with him at the hospital; everyone is pushing for the officer to be treated right away. Five minutes later, the criminal who shot him is also brought to the ER, having been shot by the policeman. He is in much greater need of an operation. The doctor on duty orders two operating rooms, but only one is available.

YOU BE THE JUDGE: *Should the doctor give the operating room to the criminal, who needs the operation more and whose life is in greater danger, or to the policeman, who is not a criminal and whose family is present, encouraging the doctor to treat him right away?*

The Answer to Cops and Robbers

Who gets the surgery when only one room is available?

[a] Of course, there is a general mitzvah to save the life of as many people as possible. Even if the person is not an upstanding individual, he or she is created "in the image of God"—*b-tzelem elohim*. However, in our case, when only one operating room is available, the doctor must choose whom to save.

Common sense logic tells us to save the policeman since 1) he is the more moral person and 2) he will continue to save lives if he survives, while the criminal might continue to hurt others. But common sense and logic are not always the guiding principles when it comes to defining Jewish law and values.

[b] Even though it is clear to us that the man is the perpetrator of a crime, no person or doctor may act as a judge and pronounce the person guilty prior to a legal trial. This basic concept familiar to us as "innocent until proven guilty" is based on a verse in the Torah (Numbers 35:12) which states that punishment cannot be administered until after a trial. Maimonides (*Hilkhot Rotzeah* 1:5) says that no punishment may be administered by witnesses (even if they are judges by profession) at the scene of a crime, until a person has gone through the entire legal process. Would the doctor, by choosing the policeman, already be pronouncing judgment on the alleged criminal?

[c] The Talmud (*Sanhedrin* 74a) teaches that a person is not permitted to say, or even to believe, that one person's "blood is redder than another's." This means no human being is capable of judging who is more valuable than whom. We cannot truly see inside a person to evaluate all of the conditions that led to particular behaviors. Only God can do this. Therefore, the doctor cannot decide who gets the operation room based on past behavior or higher morality.

[d] The Talmud discusses a case like ours (*Sanhedrin* 32b). Two identical boats are travelling in opposite directions, trying to cross a narrow channel, which has room for only one boat. The first option should be compromise. Failing that, the boat that is closer, that arrived first, goes first. In our case, where compromise is impossible, the policeman should therefore be taken to the operating room because he arrived first. However, the case of the boats is predicated on the situation where the needs are identical, but in our case the needs are not identical.

[e] The person in greater danger of losing life always takes precedence, based on the dictum (*Ketubot* 12b), "a sure thing versus a possible thing–a sure thing is preferred." (Here the "sure thing" is the need for the operation in order to survive). Therefore, although intuitively we may WANT to save the policeman, the criminal should get the operating room, since both his need and his danger are greater.

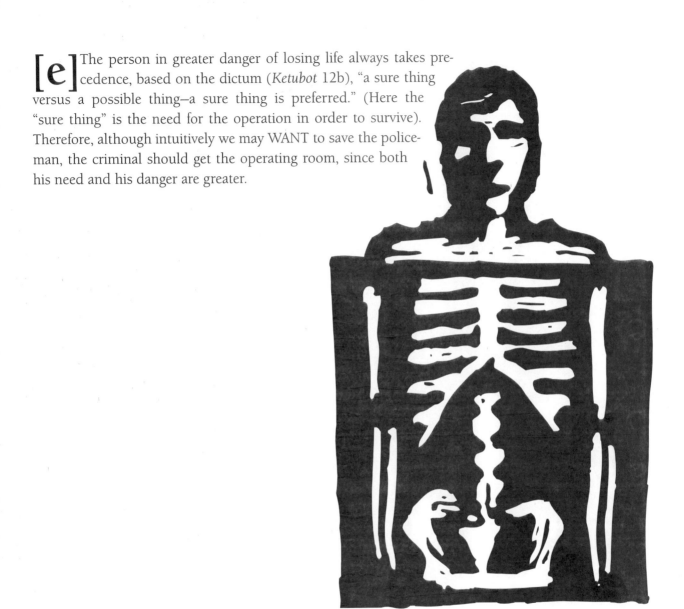

[22] Fists or Formalities

Michael, a law-abiding citizen, is walking in the city with his girlfriend and proudly wearing a *Magen David* around his neck. Suddenly, a large man starts mocking Michael and his girlfriend because they are Jewish. Speaking right at them, he utters phrases like "Hitler was right," and "Make Jews into lampshades." Michael has the urge to hit the man, even if he may be hurt in the fight. He does not want the man to "get away" with such attacks against Jews. On the other hand, Michael knows that starting a fight is against the law. He also knows that there is a police station a block and a half away where he could file a complaint.

YOU BE THE JUDGE: *Is it justified, as a Jew, to ever physically stop someone from doing something illegal? When the attack is verbal and anti-Semitic does that change anything?*

The Answer to Fists or Formalities

May one take the law into one's own hands? What if it is to react violently to personal anti-Semitism—does that change anything?

[a] Based on a casual glance at the stories in the Torah, we cannot draw any conclusions based on the evidence. On the one hand, Shimon and Levi, who destroyed the city of Shekhem following the kidnapping and rape of their sister Dinah, were strongly castigated by their father, Jacob (Genesis 34: 30). On the other hand, when idol worshippers perpetrated a great sin causing a plague that left 24,000 dead, Pinhas took the law into his own hands and killed them on the spot. When he did so, he stopped the plague and was praised for his actions (Numbers 25:10-13). What, then, is the correct reaction?

[b] When it comes to one's property, there is disagreement whether one can seize it back when it has been stolen. The law codes (*Shulhan Arukh, Hoshen Mishpat* 4) follow Rav Nahman's opinion in the Talmud (*Bava Kamma* 27b) that one *can* seize property that has been stolen (especially when retrieval through lawful means is impossible), although Rabbi Yehudah disagrees. But this case is not similar to our question.

[c] Based on the story of Pinhas, Maimonides codified the times when it is permitted to take the law into one's own hands (*Hilkhot Issurei Biah* 12:4-5) There are four specific conditions which must be adhered to in reacting violently to hurt or destroy the guilty party: 1) It must be a public desecration of God's name (usually before at least ten Jews); 2) It must take place in the heat of the moment, as an immediate reaction to the act, and not premeditated; 3) One may not consult or ask a Jewish legal authority for permission to commit such an act; 4) If the person who acts outside the law is injured or killed, relatives may not take legal action against the other party. Therefore, returning to our case, it may indeed be proper or permissible to fight or use physical force against the anti-Semite if the above conditions are adhered to.

[d] However, in general, the Jewish legal principle *Dina D'malkhuta Dina* covers this situation. *Dina D'malkhuta Dina* means "The Law of the Land" is the law. Unless (a) he would be at risk, or (b) unless that was a direct and significant danger to other people that would override the limits of local law, Michael would not be allowed to respond at that time.

[23] Your Prime Minister or Your Life...

Imagine that a terrorist armed with a bomb manages somehow to elude Israeli security and enters the Knesset with all 120 members present. He says that he really only wants to kill the Prime Minister (in another room). There is virtually no chance of overpowering the terrorist before he can detonate the bomb. If the Israelis give him the Prime Minister, he will let the rest go. If not, he will blow up the entire Knesset including the Prime Minister and the other 119 members. May one take the law into one's own hands? What if it is to react violently to personal anti-Semitism—does that change anything?

YOU BE THE JUDGE: *Should the Knesset members give the Prime Minister to the terrorist or not?*

The Answer to Your Prime Minister or Your Life...

Should the Knesset members give up the Prime Minister to the terrorist or die themselves, along with the Prime Minister? On the surface, it seems like a simple decision: saving 119 lives and giving up one life is certainly preferable to losing 120 lives. However, the Jewish value on life makes the decision much less clear.

[a] We are aware that it is written (*Sanhedrin* 37a) that "he who saves one life, it is as if he has saved an entire world." Thus, each life has the value of a world—each life has infinite value. If one life has the value of infinity, then 120 lives *also* have the value of infinity (since any number multiplied by infinity is still infinity). Therefore, based on the math and the general concept, it is not clear that 120 lives are more valuable than one life.

[b] Another Talmudic passage (*Sanhedrin* 74a) presents the case of a terrorist who puts a gun to your head, and orders you to kill another person or be killed. One may not kill another person in that instance, even to save one's own life. The Talmud asks, "Who says that your blood is redder than his blood?" suggesting that no person can judge whose life is more valuable than whose. By extension, we may ask, "Who says that any two or five people are more valuable than any one person?"

[C] It is for these reasons that Maimonides (*Hilkhot Yesodai ha-Torah* 5:5) brings down our case, and rules that the Knesset members would not be allowed to save their lives by giving the terrorists "just" the Prime Minister to be killed. A person may not do anything to bring about the death of another human being. The fact that the terrorists will kill is their problem, and they will suffer for it, but any law-abiding Jew is forbidden to assist in killing. Maimonides does bring one caveat, however. If the Prime Minister (or the specific person being requestes) is guilty of sins requiring his death, then (and only then) he may be handed over to the terrorists. Short of that, nothing should be done, even if it means the death of everyone.

[24] My Bags Are Packed...Am I Ready To Go?

Mr. Weiss earns a comfortable living, gives ten percent of his income to *tzedakah*, spends time learning Torah, and spends a great deal of time with his family. He has an opportunity in a new job to earn four times this amount. However, this would entail much travel, separating him from his family for extended periods. The additional income would also allow Mr. Weiss to give four times the *tzedakah*, but would curtail his Torah learning.

YOU BE THE JUDGE: *Should Mr. Weiss accept or reject this offer?*

The Answer to My Bags Are Packed...Am I Ready To Go?

Should one forgo Torah-learning time and family time to earn more money, in order to give more to *tzedakah*?

[a] First, it should be noted that the mitzvah of *tzedakah* does not have a fixed amount, by way of a total to give each year. It is based on a percentage formula. The *Shulhan Arukh* (*Yoreh Deah* 299:1) rules that one is supposed to give between ten percent and twenty of one's income to *tzedakah*. Therefore, Mr. Weiss already fulfills his obligation (minimally) by giving ten percent of his income. He would not be doing a greater mitzvah if he increased his income fourfold and gave four times the *tzedakah*, since he would continue to give the same percentage.

[b] While it is nice to help those in need, Judaism is not so interested in people giving vast amounts of *tzedakah*. One is FORBIDDEN to give more than twenty percent of one's income, lest this make this person poor himself (*Rema* on *Shulhan Arukh, Yoreh Deah* 249:1). Thus, merely increasing the amount one gives or increasing the percentage of *tzedakah* (beyond twenty percent) is not a very Jewish idea.

[c] Regarding the great value of giving *tzedakah* versus the values of Torah learning, Judaism believes that the world stands upon three pillars: Torah, Service to God, and Kindness. (*Tzedakah* falls into this last category.) Thus, all three values are needed by the world and by each Jew. Furthermore, after death, when one is about to face the Almighty, each person will be asked a series of questions about his or her life. One is not asked how much *tzedakah* he or she gave. Rather, the first three questions will be (*Shabbat* 31a): 1) Were you honest in business dealings? 2) Did you set aside time for Torah learning? 3) Did you spend your time with your children and insure that they will grow up properly? Therefore, based on these questions, we can clearly see that, in a certain sense, Torah and family are more important than earning extra income in order to give more to *tzedakah*.

Based on all the above sources and ideas, it is clear that Mr. Weiss, as a Jew, should not take the new job for the reasons he proposed.

[25] Independence Day

Josh Schnitzer was born in early June, and his thirteenth birthday comes (in the Jewish and secular calendars) during the second week of June. Josh's parents feel that making a party to celebrate his becoming a bar mitzvah at that time is inconvenient. Josh and his brother have end-of-the-year exams in school, not all of the relatives from across the country could attend at that time, and all the "good" halls are booked for June weddings. They want to postpone the celebration of becoming a bar mitzvah until the July 4 weekend, when it is convenient for everyone and they can get the best catering hall in town.

YOU BE THE JUDGE: *Is it right for them also to delay Josh's coming to the Torah in shul for this convenience?*

The Answer to Independence Day

Should the convenience of leading the service and having the party on the same day take precedence here?

[**a**] Becoming a bar or bat mitzvah is a blessed event in life. A child celebrates his or her first *aliyah* to the Torah and first Torah/Haftarah reading at this time, when he becomes 13 and she becomes 12 (in a traditional setting). Indeed, it should make no difference when that first time takes place *vis a vis* a person's birthday. The Mishnah, though, (*Avot* 5:5) speaks of certain ages in a person's life at which certain events should take place. For example, at the age of 5, a child is capable of, and should begin, learning the Written Torah. The Mishnah continues and says that at the age of 13 (for a boy), he begins performing mitzvot (as commandments and not as voluntary acts). Why at this specific age? We know that the performance of an act is predicated on the concept of free choice. Rabbinic "instructions" about the appropriate age at which to accept the mitzvot may come because of the Jewish view of free will. Until a person has a completely developed free choice (i.e., an equal good and evil inclination), true choice is impossible.

[**b**] The Talmud (*Sanhedrin* 91b) states that the evil inclination (*yetzer ha-rah*) in a human being exists either before birth or by the moment of birth. The good inclination (*yetzer ha-tov*), however, is not fully developed until a boy is 13 or a girl is 12 years old (*Avot DeRabbi Natan* 16:2). Thus, true free will in Judaism is a sort of "coming of age." The celebration of becoming a bar or a bat mitzvah is actually a celebration of a particular development within us. The celebration is not primarily about the performance of Jewish skills. Technically, a Jew becomes a bar or bat mitzvah on his or her Hebrew birthday, even if he or she never does anything in the synagogue! By 12 and 13 (for girls and boys, respectively) free will becomes fully active, and thus we have a right to celebrate our becoming b'nai mitzvah, children of the commandments.

[**c**] If this is the basis of celebration, then we can understand the celebration of the *day* to be far more important than the celebration of any religious act such as an *aliyah* or Torah reading. It is for this reason that, unlike the custom in the Western world, the common practice in Israel is to celebrate the bar or bat mitzvah with a party on the precise evening of the child's twelfth or thirteenth birthday according

to the Jewish calendar, even if it is a week night. Only after this party, on the following Shabbat, does the child get an *aliyah* or read the Torah or Haftarah.

Returning to our question, we now understand that it is preferred to celebrate on the day that a boy turns 13 or a girl 12, or a day close to it, despite any inconvenience. Of course, it is not forbidden to celebrate later (if circumstances make it difficult or impossible to celebrate at the correct time), just as many people sometimes celebrate an anniversary or birthday long after the event.

[26] If a Tree Falls in the Forest...

After ecologists showed that cutting down the old growth forests in the northwest United States is harmful to the area's ecology, a movement has developed to force the wood companies to stop cutting these trees. However, this would result in the loss of hundreds of jobs and affect thousands of people.

YOU BE THE JUDGE: *Does preserving these trees justify the negative effects on thousands of people? Is preserving the ecological balance of plants and animals more important than the lives of thousands of people?*

The Answer to If a Tree Falls in the Forest...

Should trees be preserved for ecological reasons if it means the loss of hundreds of jobs? Consider the following:

[a] Judaism places a high value upon ecological concerns. Even before the term ecology was invented, Judaism reflected an environmental consciousness. In the Torah, when Adam is first commanded regarding his relationship with the earth, he is told to "WORK IT AND TO PRESERVE IT" (Genesis 2: 15). Additionally, the Torah prohibits planting or building within 1000 cubits of the city limits (Numbers 35:2), and Rashi explains (based on *Bava Metzia* 24b) that the reason for this ordinance is to maintain the physical beauty of the city. The Mishnah (*Bava Batra* 2:8) discusses and forbids air pollution, and the *Shulhan Arukh* (*Hoshen Mishpat* 412:5) forbids certain types of water pollution.

[b] While permitting the Israelites to cut down trees (Deuteronomy 20:19-20), God commands that one may not cut down a fruit tree merely for its wood. If one did cut down a fruit tree, it would fall in the list of transgressions that have to do with being a *Bal Tash-hit*, someone who destroys and creates needless destruction in the world. (Maimonides, *Hilkhot Melakhim* 6:8). If however, it is necessary and serves a purpose, then "the earth's destruction" is permitted in Judaism. So, for example, Maimonides rules that one *may* cut down a fruit tree that is doing damage to other trees (and of course use it for wood or paper).

[c] One issue related to our above case involves the damage that cutting down such trees can do to the planet. If it could be shown that cutting down trees poses a direct danger to human existence on earth, then this concern would supercede all others, and it would be forbidden to cut down the trees (Deuteronomy 4:9, 15).

[d] Regarding the specific question about the trees versus the negative effects on workers, the main issue is whether maintaining jobs is considered a legitimate human need. Although not referring to our circumstances directly, the *Shulhan Arukh* (*Hoshen Mishpat* 155:22) rules that even when trees should be cut down, the workers are entitled to monetary compensation if they are deprived from work as a result, because they were legitimately working before the ecological problem was detected or discovered.

This seems to imply that when ecology prevents the logging of certain woodlands, the workers are entitled to compensation for their loss of jobs.

[e] Jewish sensitivity to long-range environmental problems is spelled out in a midrash (*Kohelet Rabbah* 7:20). The midrash says that at the beginning of Creation, God put Adam in the Garden and showed him all the vegetables and animals that were created. He asked Adam to note how beautiful and good they are, and how they were all put on the earth for people. But then God warned Adam, telling him to be careful not to damage these creations, because this could ultimately cause the world to be destroyed. Once it is destroyed, says God, the damage is irreparable.

[27] Twentieth Century Foxes

Recently, fox hunting has come under attack in England, and there is a proposal to ban it. In the United States, many hunters take pride in this sport and defend their right to hunt foxes.

YOU BE THE JUDGE: *If a person truly enjoys the sport of hunting, is it morally right to hunt and kill animals?*

The Answer to Twentieth Century Foxes

Is hunting a legitimate and moral pursuit in Judaism?

[a] It is important to remember that Judaism stresses sensitivity to animals. On the one hand, the first commandment given to Adam is to rule over the fish, birds and animals, signifying that human beings can use animals for their own needs (Genesis 1:28). This implies that we are permitted to hunt animals. Later on, after the Flood, this relationship is spelled out even more clearly, as God tells man (Genesis 9:2) that animals will fear human beings, and that all creatures have been given over into people's hands for their needs. On the other hand, people may not needlessly hurt animals. As Jews, we are commanded to help unload an animal whose burden is too heavy, even if it belongs to an enemy (Exodus 23:5). In addition, the Torah spells out a great sensitivity to the "feelings" of animals (Deuteronomy 22:10, 25:4, Leviticus 22:28). For instance, it says, "YOU SHALL NOT MUZZLE AN OX...(Deuteronomy 25:4) This implies that hunting is not permitted, but that is the normative Jewish outlook regarding hunting?

[b] Consistent with Judaism's view regarding the use of the earth and its vegetation by man, God has only permitted man to use animals if the need is legitimate, if no unnecessary pain is inflicted, and if nothing unnecessary is wasted. Therefore, for example, a Jew is permitted to eat meat (since the need is legitimate) and kill animals for food (since that is necessary for eating meat), but only through *shekhita* (ritual slaughter), since that inflicts the least amount of pain in killing an animal (*Sefer Ha-Hinuch*, Mitzvah 451).

[c] In the Talmud, Rabbi Shimon (*Avodah Zara* 18b) castigates anyone who takes part in something called *kangiyon*. Rashi's comments explain that this activity is hunting for animals, using dogs, purely for pleasure. This sounds very close to fox hunting. Therefore, we see that Judaism indeed frowns upon hunting for pleasure, and does not consider it a legitimate human need. Even when the Mishnah uses the term normally translated as hunting—*metzudah*—it clearly refers to trapping with nets only, without hurting the animal. Indeed, this reference only permits trapping animals for food, and not for pleasure. Many centuries later, Rav Yehudah Landau codified this general Jewish attitude in his *Responsa Noda Biyehudah* (*Yoreh Deah* 10) and clearly forbade Jews to hunt for pleasure.

[28] Should We Let the Home Run Kings Run Away from Home?

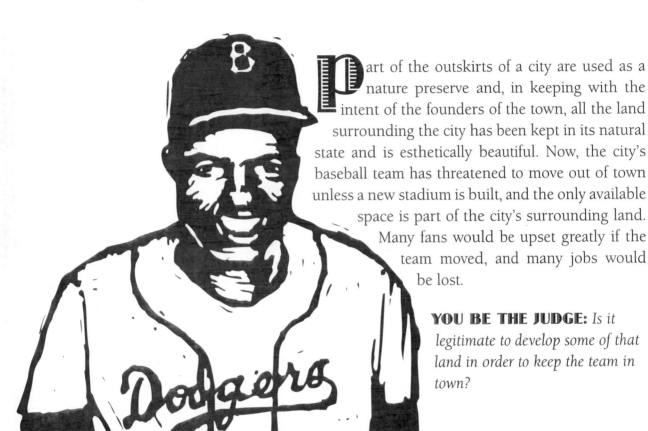

Part of the outskirts of a city are used as a nature preserve and, in keeping with the intent of the founders of the town, all the land surrounding the city has been kept in its natural state and is esthetically beautiful. Now, the city's baseball team has threatened to move out of town unless a new stadium is built, and the only available space is part of the city's surrounding land. Many fans would be upset greatly if the team moved, and many jobs would be lost.

YOU BE THE JUDGE: *Is it legitimate to develop some of that land in order to keep the team in town?*

73

The Answer to Should We Let the Home Run Kings Runaway from Home?

Should the city destroy some of its natural, beautiful surrounding lands in order to keep the local baseball team in town and prevent fans from becoming upset?

[a] This situation presents two competing values, both of which are significant in Judaism. The economy and the preservation of jobs are both important aspects of society in Judaism's eyes. For example, a person may not open up a competing store next to an existing store, if it will drive the first store out of business (Deuteronomy 19:14). On the other hand, a city's beauty and its preservation are also important in Judaism.

[b] Jerusalem was not only praised as the most holy and spiritual city (*Mishnah Kelim* 1:7), but also for her beauty. The Midrash (*Esther Rabbah* 1:16) tells us that of the ten measures of physical beauty in the world, Jerusalem received nine. The Torah also desires that the beauty of every city be preserved and, therefore, prohibits using the outskirts of a city for planting, grazing or for financial considerations (Numbers 25:2). Rashi's comments on this verse explain that the goal of this prohibition is to guarantee the city's beauty. Given these conflicting values, what does Judaism say about our question?

[c] In codifying the Jewish law based on the verse quoted above, Maimonides (*Hilkhot Shabbat Veyovail* 13:1-5) states that, "The reserved areas around the city have been explained in the Torah as consisting of 3,000 cubits in all directions from the walls of the city outwards... The first 1,000 is a reserved area and the 2,000 cubits from there outwards are for fields and vineyards." Rabbi Samson Raphael Hirsch, the famous modern Bible commentator, in commenting on the same verse, says that the main purpose of these laws is to limit the size of urban areas and to prevent the building of mega-cities. However, Maimonides has written that these laws *only apply to cities in Israel*. Therefore, an American city that wants to use its outskirts for a stadium is not violating any Jewish law, although it may violate the "spirit of the law."

What about an Israeli soccer team which desired to move outside their city? In Israel, oftentimes even ancient Jewish law prevails.

[29] How Deep is Skin Deep?

Susan has always been very attractive and has had many boys attracted to her because of her beauty. In addition, because of Susan's popularity with boys, many girls befriended Susan as well. Another girl, Rachel, is not that attractive but has many friends (although not as many as Susan). When Susan and Rachel talk, Rachel says that she is jealous of Susan because of her great popularity. However, Susan says she is jealous of Rachel because Rachel knows that her friends are true friends, and do not befriend her simply because of outer beauty.

YOU BE THE JUDGE: *Is it better to be Susan or Rachel? Why?*

The Answer to How Deep is Skin Deep?

Should we aspire to physical beauty? Is inner beauty all that matters?

[a] The Talmud describes four very righteous women as being exceedingly attractive (*Megillah* 15a). Here, their qualities as God-fearing and kind made them beautiful, yet the Gemara does note that they were physically attractive as well. Even the physical beauty of non-Jewish people is admired. When Rabban Gamliel was on the steps outside the Temple, he saw a beautiful woman who was also an idol worshipper. Nonetheless, he commented about how beautiful she was. Another sage commented that one should recite a blessing when seeing such beauty (*Avodah Zara* 20a). Thus, we see that Judaism admires physical beauty.

[b] However, the Talmud also says that Rabbi Akiva cried when he saw the great beauty of the Roman general Turnusrufus (*Avodah Zara* 20a). The Talmud explains that Rabbi Akiva cried because he realized that this great beauty would eventually dissipate. For this reason, physical beauty is not regarded as highly as other values (wisdom, for example). King Solomon goes as far as to write that all physical beauty is worthless (Proverbs 31:30). How, then, can Judaism admire beauty and at the same time believe it to be worthless?

[c] One of the answers resolving this apparent contradiction will also help resolve our case. Beauty is considered worthless when it stands alone, when it is the only value a person possesses. When combined with other values, however, beauty is quite positive. The metaphor is that the numerical value of something worthless is zero, but if another number of value is placed before the zero, the combined value is enhanced ten times because of that zero. Thus, if Susan's only virtue is her beauty, then it has little or no value by itself. But if Susan also has other positive qualities, then these are enhanced by her physical attractiveness.

[d] We also learn (*Pirke Avot* 4:20) that one should not only look at the outside of a wine flask, since there are unattractive flasks with great contents and extremely attractive flasks with nothing at all inside. (Our expression is "Do not judge a book by its cover.") Based on this Mishnah, we understand that the inner beauty of a person is far more important that the outer beauty. However, we can infer from this Mishnah that if a person has both a beautiful inside *and* outside (physical attractiveness), then this supersedes mere inner beauty.

[e] Finally, in speaking about a love relationship, the Mishnah (*Avot* 5:6) says that if a relationship is based on only one thing (i.e., physical beauty) then the relationship will fall apart when that one thing disappears (as beauty must). But if the relationship is not based on any one thing, then it will endure forever. Therefore, if people only befriend Susan for her beauty, that type of relationship will not endure. But, based on the sources above, if Susan possesses other good qualities in addition to physical beauty, then physical attractiveness is definitely an asset.

[30] Truth or Consequences

rs. Davis goes shopping and she sees a dress that she thinks is absolutely beautiful. In addition, the dress is on sale. However, a condition of the sale is that there are no returns or exchanges. Mrs. Davis eagerly buys the dress. Later that night, when she puts on the dress, Mr. Davis thinks it looks horrendous. He does not say anything, but when Mrs. Davis asks him how it looks on her, he is in a quandary. Mr. Davis tries never to lie. However, if he tells his wife the truth, he knows that she will be very upset.

YOU BE THE JUDGE: *What should he do?*

The Answer to Truth or Consequences

Should a husband lie to his wife and tell her that her new dress is really beautiful when he believes the dress looks horrendous? We know that it is wrong, in general, to lie about anything. However, no man wants to upset his wife needlessly, especially when she cannot return the dress. What, then, should the husband do?

[a] In Judaism, lying is clearly forbidden. Not only is it generally forbidden to lie (Leviticus 19:11), this is the only sin that a Jew is specifically commanded to run away from (Exodus 23:7). In fact, telling the truth is so important that the Talmud says (*Shabbat* 55a) that God's signature is *emet* (truth). Truth is also one of the three pillars upon which the world stands (*Avot* 1:18). Thus, lying is certainly antithetical to Judaism.

[b] However, the prohibition of lying is not absolute. In certain circumstances, Judaism permits a person to tell a "white lie" in order to achieve peace (*Yevamot* 65b). This suggests that it may be permissible for a husband to lie to his wife about her new dress, in order to keep peace between them. How far does this exception extend? The example found in the Talmud that most closely mirrors our question is the case of a bride and groom at their wedding (*Ketubot* 16b). It is a special mitzvah to dance before the bride and make her happy. The Talmud (*Ketubot* 16b) asks the question: Must a person, while dancing before the bride, say that she is beautiful? Since some brides are not beautiful, is this not a lie? Beit Shammai is of the opinion that a person may not say that the bride is beautiful, but, rather, should describe her as "as beautiful as she is" (so as not to distinguish between the truly beautiful brides and less beautiful brides). Beit Hillel argues and says that a person should call *every* bride beautiful and graceful. In discussing the reasoning for his opinion, Beit Hillel brings up our question: When someone has made a bad purchase at the market, says Hillel, you still praise it. Here is our case!

[c] The *Shulhan Arukh* (*Even ha-Ezer* 65:1) rules according to Beit Hillel, agreeing that every bride should be called beautiful and graceful.

If we agree with Hillel that it is sometimes necessary to watch what we say in order to protect others' feelings, we must explain the reasoning for this allowance. First, we must realize that, according to the *Arukh Le-Nair* commentary, the Torah never says that a complete lie is permissible. The only type of lie that is permitted is a statement which is true in a certain sense. For example, to the groom, the bride is indeed beautiful, and even if not physically, she is beautiful to everyone in other ways. In our case, the dress is indeed beautiful—to the wife. Second, according to the *Reshash* commentary, lying is only permitted in a case when it will not make any practical difference. It makes no difference whether the husband says or does not say that the dress is beautiful, since it cannot be returned in any case. Similarly, calling a bride beautiful makes no practical difference. Only these types of lies are permitted, and only under special circumstances, as outlined in the Codes of Jewish Law.

Therefore, in our case, the husband is indeed permitted to say the dress is beautiful, but only because the dress is not returnable. However, he should make an effort to admire the dress in a way that is not an outright lie or not a lie at all (for example "Your dress is one of a kind.").

[31] The Ethics of Dwarf Tossing

number of years ago, a new activity became popular in a number of bars: dwarf tossing. People would take turns throwing dwarfs as far as they could to see who would win the contest. There was padding and the dwarfs readily volunteered since they were paid well.

YOU BE THE JUDGE: *If the danger was minimal and the dwarfs agreed to take part, is there anything wrong with such an activity?*

The Answer to The Ethics of Dwarf Tossing

Is it permitted to hold dwarf-tossing contests if the dwarfs themselves agree to participate? Most dwarfs do not mind participating in such contests because they are paid well. But if we were to go deeper and investigate the inner feelings of these dwarfs, we would discover that they certainly feel degraded by taking part in such activities. Therefore, the real question is whether it is permitted to degrade someone if he or she agrees to it

[a] The Midrash (*Bereshit Rabbah* 24:7) says that every time a person embarrasses another, the person and God are diminished. Since people are created in God's image, the transgression has a double effect. If this is the actual reason behind the prohibition against embarrassing others, then we can also understand why it is also forbidden for a person to embarrass him or herself. Embarrassing or cursing oneself *also* diminishes the image of God, and is therefore forbidden (Mishnah, *Shavuot* 4:13).

[b] In addition, it is forbidden to cause intentional harm to one's body (Maimonides, *Hilkhot Rotzeah* 1:4) not only because this diminishes the image of God, but also since one's body belongs to God and not to any human being. For both of these reasons, a dwarf, or any other human being, may not allow him/herself to be intentionally hurt, either physically or emotionally, as part a game for the entertainment of paying customers.

[c] The prohibition against embarrassing someone (or oneself) is so severe that it carries a punishment that even eclipses the sentence of a murderer. While a murderer is often punished in this world by the loss of life, the result of embarrassing someone is the loss of life in the Next World, a far greater punishment (Maimonides, *Hilkhot Hovail u'Mazik* 5:7).

[d] The lengths to which Judaism goes to avoid embarrassment are indeed great. The Torah (Leviticus 6:18) mentions that the place in the Temple where the burnt offering is brought is the same place that the sin offering is brought. The Talmud (*Sotah* 32b) explains that the Torah legislated this in order to protect the identity of those who sinned and were commanded to bring a sin offering. By having both groups bring their sacrifices in the same place, no one could distinguish the sinners by looking at a particular place in the Temple. Similarly, we recite the essential prayer in Judaism, the *Shmoneh Esrei*, in silence, because (among other reasons) we do not wish to embarrass those Jews who enumerate their sins during the course the prayer (*Sotah* 32b).

[32] Gramma Sara's Plug

Great-Grandma Sara is 91 years old. She is suffering from a debilitating illness, and the doctors have said that she will never recover. The cost of her hospital stay is $10,000 per month and it is draining her life savings, which would have been her family's inheritance. She is of sound mind and is in constant, but not overwhelming, pain. Because of the great medical expense and because of her inheritance, she asks her family to petition the hospital to "pull the plug" and remove her from the machines that are keeping her alive.

YOU BE THE JUDGE: *Should the family listen to her wishes?*

The Answer to Gramma Sara's Plug

Are considerations about money for end-stage medical treatments valid under Jewish law? Lay a dying person weigh between providing an inheritance for his or her children and paying the medical bills? May he or she then decide that paying for medical care is not worth the expense and request that the doctors pull the plug?

[a] In general, Judaism believes that it is not up to a person to decide to end his or her life, since that life does not belong to the person at all, but rather to God (Maimonides, *Hilkhot Rotzeah* 1:4). This is also one of the reasons that we are commanded to keep ourselves as healthy as possible and out of danger (Deuteronomy 15:9&15), and are also forbidden to harm ourselves (*Bava Kama* 90b). Since our bodies are merely "on loan" to us from God, we must treat them as any borrowed object should be treated: with the greatest care not to be damaged or destroyed.

[b] Specific to the concept of life, Judaism not only believes that each life is equal to the entire world— i.e. an infinite worth (*Sanhedrin* 37a)—but also that every minute of life is infinite and is equal to the entire world (infinity divided by any number is still infinity). Therefore, the man who aided King Saul to die just a few minutes early (at Saul's request), is condemned in the Bible as a murderer (II Samuel 1: 9-16). In general, one is not permitted to violate Shabbat except when there is a possibility of saving a life. However, if a dying person (collapsed under rubble, for example) could be kept alive for just a few more hours through the violation of Shabbat (i.e., removing the rubble), then a Jew is not only permitted, but even obligated to violate Shabbat for this purpose (*Shulhan Arukh, Orekh Hayyim* 329:3-5). This shows that even a few hours of life have the value of an entire life. Thus, shortening any life, even by a few hours, is tantamount to destroying an entire life.

[c] It is said that when Rabbi Hananya ben Tradyon was being burned at the hands of the Romans, his students begged him to open his mouth, so that he would die more quickly. He refused, however, since that would have shortened his life by a few moments (*Avoda Zara* 18a).

[d] Thus, Great-Grandma Sara, or any other person, is forbidden to end her life "early," even to relieve suffering (Maimonides, *Hilkhot Rotzeah* 2:7). Certainly, any financial consideration, no matter how substantial, cannot possibly be equated with even a moment of life. Only God, not people, may determine the moment of death (*Pesaḥim* 54b).

However, when one is already close to death, it is not necessary to intervene and maintain his/her life.

[e] There is one story in the Talmud (*Ketubot* 104a) which relates what happened on the day that Rabbi Judah was dying. The Rabbis decreed a public fast and offered prayer for heavenly mercy so that Rabbi Judah would not die. Rabbi Judah's handmaid saw how he suffered...she ascended to the roof and prayed for him to die. The Rabbis continued their prayers for heavenly mercy, and the handmaid took a jar and threw it down from the roof to the ground. When the rabbis heard the sound of the jar shattering, they stopped praying for a moment and the soul of Rabbi Judah departed.

[f] Rabbenu Nissim (commentary to *Nedarim* 40a), said that sometimes one must request mercy on behalf of the ill so that he might die, as in the case of a patient who is terminal and who is in great pain.

[g] It happened that a woman who had aged considerably appeared before Rabbi Yose ben Halafta. She said, 'Rabbi, I am much too old. Life has become a burden for me. I can no longer taste food or drink. I wish to die.' Rabbi Yose asked her, 'To what do you ascribe your longevity?' She answered that it was her habit to pray in the synagogue every morning, and despite occasional, more pressing needs she never had missed a service. Rabbi Yose advised her to refrain from attending services for three consecutive days. She heeded his advice and on the third day she took ill and died. (*Yalkut Shimoni*, Proverbs 943)

In general, we are allowed to do nothing that will cause death, but can allow someone who is in pain to die naturally.

[33] Wrapped in Controversy

Recently, a furor was created by activists who protested against the use of trapped and 'tortured' animals in the making of fur coats. Despite the protests, many women today still prefer to wear fur coats because 1) they are warmer than synthetic fur, and 2) they are more of a status symbol than synthetic fur. A particular woman wants to wear a fur coat, claiming that animals are killed for many utilitarian reasons including food and leather production. Even some of the people who protest making fur coats out of real animals wear leather belts and eat meat, she says.

YOU BE THE JUDGE: *Is it morally right to wear the fur coat? Does it make a difference if the animals were bred on a farm and killed painlessly?*

The Answer to Wrapped in Controversy

Can a person wear fur that was obtained by trapping animals?

[a] In Judaism, there is great sensitivity to animals' needs and feelings, especially when it comes to pain. For example, a verse from the *Shema* (Deuteronomy 11:15) reads, "I WILL PROVIDE GRASS IN YOUR FIELD FOR YOUR CATTLE AND YOU WILL EAT AND BE SATISFIED." In this verse, the needs of animals are mentioned before those of people. Based on this verse, the Talmud (*Gittin* 62a) and the Mishnah Torah (Maimonides' Code, *Hilkhot Avadim* 9:8) rule that people must feed their animals before eating.

[b] The Torah is also explicit regarding an animal's pain, whether physical or psychological. It demands (Deuteronomy 25:4) that a hungry animal not be muzzled as it works in the field. It must be allowed to eat freely of the crops (even at a loss to the owner) while it works in the field. This law stems from the same reasoning as the law which states that people are allowed to eat in the fields while they harvest crops, explains Rabbenu Baḥya. Desire occurs in animals, just as it does in humans, and it would be unfair if we demanded that they refrain from eating the crops that they are working to harvest.

[c] Two different types of animals, such as a donkey and an ox, may not plow the field together, since, according to *Sefer ha-Ḥinukh* (*Mitzvah* 503) two different species will plow at different speeds and cause pain to each other. An animal and its offspring may not be slaughtered on the same day (Leviticus 22:28), so that a parent need not witness the death of its offspring. Similarly, a mother bird may not watch as its eggs are being taken away: "YOU SHALL SURELY SEND AWAY THE MOTHER AND TAKE THE YOUNG FOR YOUR-SELF, SO THAT IT WILL BE GOOD FOR YOU AND WILL PROLONG YOUR DAYS" (Deuteronomy 22:6-7).

[d] For the animal's sake, the Torah requires a Jew to assist anyone who is loading or unloading an animal: "IF YOU SEE THE DONKEY OF SOMEONE YOU HATE CROUCHING UNDER ITS BURDEN, WOULD YOU REFRAIN FROM HELPING HIM? YOU SHALL HELP REPEATEDLY WITH HIM" (Exodus 23:5). Since longer periods of carrying inevitably result in increased pain, the mitzvah of unloading takes precedence over the mitzvah of loading. In fact, Jewish law says that you must even help to unload your enemy's animal before loading your friend's. Here, the concern for the animal's needs takes precedence those of the human.

[e] Given all this sensitivity to animals, it is important to remember that people are permitted to use animals for their benefit. According to Genesis 1:28 animals were put on earth to serve and work for people: "...FILL THE EARTH AND SUBDUE IT; AND RULE OVER THE FISH OF THE SEA, THE BIRD OF THE SKY, AND EVERY LIVING THING THAT MOVES ON THE EARTH." Therefore, we can kill animals for things such as food and clothing. So how do these two values mesh, given the kind of attitude that we saw above? The answer is in the Jewish concept of *tza-ar baalei ḥayyim*, being respectful to animals and not causing them harm unnecessarily. While one may use animals for legitimate human need, one may not *unnecessarily* cause pain to any animal. Thus, according the *Sefer ha-Hinukh*, when one does kill an animal for food, the kosher slaughtering process is the least painful method. Even when pain can be inflicted for legitimate human need, any "extra" pain is forbidden.

[f] We can now return to our original question. If a fur coat is indeed warmer than other synthetic materials, then its use may be classified as serving a legitimate human need. If that were the case, real fur coats may be worn. If, however, the purpose of wearing fur is merely for fashion or as a status symbol, then this would not be considered a legitimate need. Rather, it is a frivolous reason, and would then be forbidden. Regarding the trapping of animals for fur, which entails maiming and "extra" pain, Judaism would encourage more humane methods of breeding and harvesting the fur.

[34] Evil Earfuls

Jamie knows that it is wrong to speak about other people, especially in a negative sense. But her friend Julie constantly talks about people and "badmouths" other girls in their class. Julie doesn't really pay attention when Jamie talks about others, but she never really does anything to stop Julie from saying these things either.

YOU BE THE JUDGE: *Is it wrong merely to hear these words, even though Jamie herself is not actually saying or doing anything?*

The Answer to Evil Earfuls

Is it improper merely to hear someone speak badly about another person? Must you do something to stop them from speaking negatively about others?

[a] In Judaism, *Lashon ha-Ra* (speaking badly about another person) is a sin, even if what is said is true. It is not only clearly forbidden in the Torah: "YOU SHALL NOT GOSSIP AMONG YOUR PEOPLE" (Leviticus 19:16), but is considered worse than idol worship (Midrash, *Yalkut Shimoni, Tehillim* 3:621). We know this from comparing two stories in the Torah. On the one hand, when the Jews sinned by creating and worshipping the Golden Calf, they were not severely punished. However, when the spies came back and badmouthed the land of Israel, having lost faith in God, the entire nation was punished by not being allowed to enter the Promised Land. The next generation would inherit the Land of Milk and Honey instead.

[b] *Lashon ha-Ra* is also equated with the three "worst" sins in Judaism: murder, idol worship and sexual impropriety, combined (Maimonides, *Hilkhot Deot* 7:3). The power of speech makes people God-like. When we use it for good purposes, we are like the Creator of the Universe, as *Pirke Avot* 5:1 reminds us: "By ten sayings was the world created...." God created the world through the spoken word, and by utilizing the spoken we can create a meaningful life. As it says in Psalms 34:13-14: WHO IS THE PERSON THAT DESIRES LIFE AND LOVES MANY DAYS, THAT HE/SHE SEE GOD? KEEP YOUR TONGUE FROM EVIL AND YOUR LIPS FROM GUILE..."

[c] Are all of the above sources about the speaker? What about the listener? The Torah gives us a clue: When Miriam spoke badly about her brother Moses, it says that "MIRIAM AND AARON SPOKE..." (Numbers 12:1), but the verb itself is singular. Although the words were physically spoken only by Miriam, the verse implies that Aaron also said the words. Why? In order to teach us that one who *hears* evil words (as Aaron did) is also guilty and as punishable as the one who actually spoke the words (as Miriam did). While it is true that the speaker receives a far worse punishment (as in the case of Miriam and Aaron), one who listens to *Lashon ha-Ra* is punished nevertheless.

[d] If no one would listen, then no one could speak any *Lashon ha-Ra*. Thus, Jamie should not remain quiet when Julie speaks *Lashon ha-Ra*. Rather, she should either ask Julie to stop speaking about others, or she should walk away. If this were to occur with all of Julie's friends, then Julie might get to a point where she was even looking for the good in others.

[35] A Killer Cure for Cancer

A doctor is very close to finding the cure for all types of cancer. However, experiments on non-human animals have proven ineffective. The only way to try out and perfect his new serum is to experiment on healthy human beings. Until the serum works at a 100% rate, about 55 people will be needed to suffer the pain of the imperfect serum and then die.

YOU BE THE JUDGE: *If no one volunteers, should the government be able "select" the people (perhaps prisoners?) in order to cure cancer forever? If so, how should they be selected?*

The Answer to A Killer Cure for Cancer

Is it ever proper to knowingly and willingly kill a few individuals (such as homeless persons or prisoners) in order to find a cure for a disease and save the lives of millions of people?

[a] The Mishnah, the earliest Rabbinic law book, says: "Whoever saves one life, it is as if he has saved the entire world." (*Sanhedrin* 4:5) This sets up a response to someone who might be thinking about using homeless people or prisoners for cancer experiments. Jewish values say that all lives are equal.

[b] Judaism believes that it is not up to people to decide the value of any one life over another. We cannot say that the life of a homeless person or that of a prisoner has less value than anyone else's life. The Talmud (*Sanhedrin* 74a) expresses this concept with the question: "Who says that your blood is redder than his blood?" This comes in response to the case of someone telling a person to kill or be killed himself. You may not kill to save your own 'red blood,' because it is worth no more than your fellow's." Each person is deemed as an equal to any other, and it is for this reason that only one human being was originally created (*Sanhedrin* 37a)—so that no one could say that "my ancestors are better than yours." Only God is the true Judge.

[c] Regarding the question of killing a few in order to save the lives of many, we know that any act of murder is one of the most serious offenses in the Torah (Exodus 20:13): "YOU SHALL NOT MURDER."It is forbidden to knowingly kill one person in order to save the life of thousands or even millions.

[d] In addition, Judaism does NOT believe that the ends justify the means. Thus, if one can do a great mitzvah, but only by committing a sin in the process, a Jew is not permitted to do such a mitzvah. It is for this reason, for example, that a stolen *lulav* is not usable for the mitzvah of shaking the four species on Sukkot (*Sukkah* 30a). Maimonides (*Hilkhot Issurei Mizbayah* 8:9) says that God detests any gift which comes about through the commission of a sin. Based on these ideas, it would be clearly forbidden to kill even one person, even a sinner, in order to develop a cure and save many more lives.

[36] Running Out of Cheeks

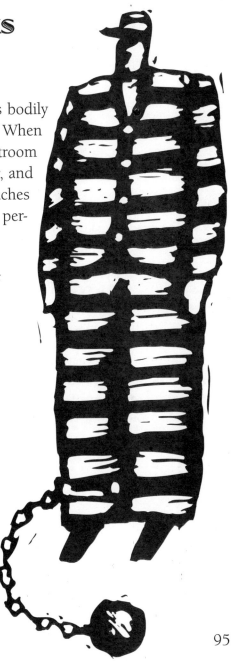

a mugger steals money from your mother and inflicts bodily harm on her. She has to spend a week in the hospital. When the mugger is caught and brought to court, you sit in the courtroom each day watching this mugger on trial. You feel rage, anger, and hatred toward this person. Traditional Christian thought teaches that a person should "turn the other cheek" and love this person.

YOU BE THE JUDGE: *Does Judaism "allow" a person to hate another human being?*

The Answer to Running Out of Cheeks

Is it permitted to hate someone who has wronged you?

[a] Many of the Jewish sources seem to indicate that we should not hate anyone. In the Torah (Leviticus 19:17) it says that one may not hate one's brother in his heart. But this raises a question: can you do it openly? A verse in the Book of Ovadiah (1:12), one of the minor prophets, says that a person may not rejoice at the fall of one's enemy. This implies that hate for one's enemy (or joy at his or her downfall) if forbidden.

[b] Hatred is such a detestable emotion that it is said that the Second Temple was destroyed because of needless hatred among Jews (*Yoma* 9b). In fact, this one sin is equated to the three big sins in Judaism: sexual impropriety, murder, and idol worship (since the First Temple was destroyed because of these sins). According to Hillel, when asked by the non-Jew to describe the essence of Judaism, he explained that what is hateful to you should not be done to anyone else (*Shabbat* 31a). The *Sefer ha-Hinuch* calls the emotion of hatred the ugliest emotion of the human race. Based on all these sources, we may conclude that hatred in Judaism is never permitted.

[c] But the famous verse from Ecclesiastics (3:8) tells us that there is "A TIME TO HATE." What do we do with that!?! When is this time? The Midrash (*Kohelet Rabbah* 3:10) explains that one may indeed hate an enemy at a time of war. But didn't we learn (codified later in the Mishnah, *Pirke Avot* 4:19) that one may not be joyous at the fall of one's enemy? The answer given is that at the time of an enemy's death, a person may not be happy, since even that enemy was created in God's image. However, *afterwards* one may indeed be happy that the enemy has fallen. Thus, it is permitted to hate someone who is an enemy of the Jews and who has repeatedly killed or harmed Jews simply because they are Jewish. But it is improper to hate others, even sinners. (See the *Hazon Ish*'s commentary on Maimonides, *Hilkhot Shekhita* 2:16.)

If the mugger is punished for what he did to you and your family, you certainly may be happy that he is receiving his just retribution. But unless he chronically harms people, it would not be permitted to continually hate this person.

[37] All For One and One For All

a teacher finds that one or more students have maliciously and seriously damaged parts of the classroom during recess, while the teacher was on a break. The teacher knows that some of the innocent students know who caused the damage, but they are refusing to tell on their friends.

YOU BE THE JUDGE: *Should the teacher use the threat of force and punishment in order to get these innocent students to reveal the culprit?*

The Answer to All For One and One For All

Is it proper for a teacher to force students to tell on those who have damaged school property?

[a] Judaism feels very strongly about preserving the right to privacy and keeping secrets (Proverbs 25:9, 20:19), forbidding the re-telling of any secret even when someone did not ask you to keep it secret. According to the author of the *Sefer Mitzvot Gedolot*, revealing any secret is a violation of a Torah sin (negative prohibition #9). Even information not specifically obtained in confidence may not be revealed (*Yoma* 4b). Nevertheless, there are certain times when a Jew is permitted or even required to reveal secret information.

[b] When summoned to testify as a witness, the Torah obligates a Jew to tell secrets and reveal everything, even if there was a previous understanding, or promise to a person, not to say anything (Leviticus 5:1; Maimonides, *Hilkhot Heviot* 5:15). In addition, if revealing secret information can help save someone's life, it is mandatory to do so (*Shulhan Arukh, Hoshen Mishpat* 426:1). Based on this source, it appears that a person must reveal a secret whenever the threat of harm to another individual is severe.

[c] Returning to our question regarding the teacher and school property, Rav Moshe Feinstein (*Igrot Moshe, Yoreh Deah* Section II, 10:34) discusses our specific case, and concludes that a teacher should not "force" students to reveal information about other students. Although the situation is certainly severe, which might lead us to allow the teacher to extract the information, Rabbi Feinstein urges the teacher to uncover the information through other means. As a teacher, he or she teaches students with every action. By "forcing" students to tell private information, it would set the wrong example by demonstrating that *Lashon ha-Ra*—"evil speech" (talking about others, repeating information, telling secrets)—is permitted. The teacher should rather speak to the students and explain the gravity of the situation, and help the guilty parties decide to come forward to admit their errors.

[38] It's Written in the Stars but Should We Read It?

a number of years ago, when it became known that First Lady Nancy Reagan consulted horoscopes and astrologers, and even based some decisions upon the information obtained, it became a scandal. Many people in high positions seem to believe that astrology can indeed predict and guide our lives.

YOU BE THE JUDGE: *Is it legitimate for Jews to consult horoscopes and/or astrologers, and then to act on the information they receive?*

The Answer to It's Written in the Stars but Should We Read It?

Are astrology and horoscopes considered valid in Judaism? Do they have a place in telling us about our lives?

[a] Surprisingly, there are many Jewish sources demonstrating how the stars, planets, and times of birth affect a person. The most famous passage is found in the Talmud (*Shabbat* 156a), where it says that a certain star causes some people to be wise, another star causes some people to be wealthy, and the list goes on. It further states that the time of one's birth (the day of the week) determines one's personality. Rabbi Hanina adds that the hour of the day in which birth occurred predicts the future of the infant.

The passage continues in a debate regarding whether or not the Jewish people have a *mazal* (a planetary influence) like other nations. The conclusion seems to be that there was a planetary influence for the Jewish people, but God changed this phenomenon. Later, on the same page of the Talmud, it is related that a non-Jewish astrologer told Rabbi Akiva (the one who said that the Jews have no planetary influences) that his daughter was in danger of being bitten by a snake. It turned out that Rabbi Akiva's daughter had performed an act of charity, and Rabbi Akiva then proclaimed that it was the act of charity that saved her from death!

[b] All of these sources are enigmatic, especially the story of Rabbi Akiva, who seems to have heeded the word of an astrologer after stating that planetary influences do not affect the Jewish people. The term we commonly use today, "*Mazal Tov*," does not technically mean "Congratulations," as most people believe, or even "Good luck." It means rather, "You have been blessed with a good planetary sign." Other sources state that the life span and friends of a person are determined by planetary influences (*Moed Katan* 38a). These statements seem to clearly indicate that Judaism does believe in astrology.

[c] Does this signify that Jews should or may consult astrologers? No! The Torah itself forbids consulting with mediums and wizards (Leviticus 19:31). Therefore, we are left with an enigma. Leviticus 19:26 says that one may not attempt to predict the future.

[d] The conflict begins to be resolved during the Gaonic period when the Gaonim, the great rabbis of the 8-10th Centuries, remark (in *Otzar ha-Gaonim* 133) that one may not view astrology as fatalistic. While astrology can give people an inclination about their lives, each person has free will to overcome this speculation.

[e] Nahmanides (in his commentary on Deuteronomy 18:13 and his Responsum 282) says that one may not *ask* an astrologer about the future (since this act is not "Jewish"—it seems to reject the Jewish idea that everything comes from God), but that a pattern of predictability does exist. Thus, if a Jew happens to overhear a prediction or information from an astrologer, one may indeed act upon this prediction. Maimonides (*Hilkhot Avodat Kokhavim* 11:8-9) emphatically disagrees with all of the above explanations, and rejects any validity at all to astrology. He says that he who believes in astrology is an ignoramus and a fool.

Therefore, while it seems that most authorities believe in some sort of astrological power, there is a fine line between believing in this and then believing in a power other than God. However, it is clear that a Jew may not consult an astrologer or medium on a regular basis.

[39] Bickering Buddies

Joey and Dave have been good friends for years. As they grow up, they find that they disagree fundamentally on many important issues such as the importance of preserving old-growth forests at the expense of jobs, beliefs in life-after-death, and simple things like saving versus spending money.

YOU BE THE JUDGE: *Can (or should) Joey and Dave try to remain good friends if they have such disagreements?*

The Answer to Bickering Buddies

Should two people remain good friends if they fundamentally disagree on many important issues? To answer this question, we must investigate the underlying concepts of friendship in Judaism.

[a] The Mishnah (*Pirke Avot* 5:16) tells us that any friendship based upon only one factor cannot possibly survive. If that one factor disappears, nothing is left. A friendship based on multiple factors, though, will endure forever. As an example, in the Mishnah we get a description of the ultimate friendship—that of Jonathan and David. These two individuals undoubtedly had many vehement disagreements. After all, it was Jonathan's father, King Saul, who viewed David as his archenemy and even tried to kill him. Through it all, David and Jonathan's friendship endured. They must have had fundamental disagreements regarding their feelings about Saul, yet they stuck it out being friends.

[b] On the other hand, if two people have different fundamental value systems and outlooks, it is very difficult to remain friends. This is true when the differences affect lifestyles, important choices and different day-to-day living patterns. Beit Shamai and Beit Hillel disagreed on many aspects of Jewish law in the pages of the Talmud, but this did not prevent their sons and daughters from marrying each other (*Yevamot* 14b) because their fundamental life choices, value systems and world-views were essentially the same. Like marriage, part of friendship is disagreeing in a respectful manner and coming to some sort of compromise whenever possible. However, if two spouses disagree about everything in their lives, the marriage will not survive.

[c] The Talmud states (*Pesaḥim* 113b) that every friendship involves hate.

[d] The Hebrew word for friend, *ḥaver*, is also the word used for a learning partner. (Today, the Aramaic form of this word is used to describe the Jewish learning process—*hevruta*.) This implies that all friendships are, in part, a learning experience. Two people learn from each other by exchanging ideas and disagreeing, making sure it is done in a respectful manner. This type of friendship is crucial in any person's development and is encouraged in Judaism. Rabina says that he learned more from his friends than he did from his teachers (*Makkot* 10a). Rabbi Eliezer says that the most important aspect of

life to "cling to" is friendship (*Avot* 3:9). When Ḥoni (the Jewish Rip van Winkle) awoke after 70 years of sleep to find that all his friends had died, he wished to die rather than to go on living (*Ta'anit* 23a).

[e] Returning to our question, if Joey and Dave have some basic values in common, then their friendship can endure and even thrive, since disagreements are healthy in a good relationship. However, if they disagree on every issue without any mutuality, then they cannot remain true friends. Always maintaining the dignity of the other person in a disagreement helps insure that we will spend life with good *ḥevrutot*—friends and learning partners.

[40] A Stitch in Time Won't Make Nine Yards

a terrible car accident occurs while a surgeon is standing close by. The driver is wedged into his seat and cannot be removed without the "Jaws of Life," which has just arrived along with other equipment. As the surgeon examines the driver, he notices two things: [1] He is a famous professional football kicker, and [2] if he waits even a few more minutes for the long process of removing him from the car, he will die. The victim's only hope is for the doctor to cut off his kicking leg, which will allow him to be evacuated immediately and possibly save his life.

YOU BE THE JUDGE: *Should the surgeon use the equipment available on the street to cut off the man's leg, or should he let him die? What if the driver is conscious and asks that the surgeon let him die, rather than face life without football?*

The Answer to A Stitch in Time Won't Make Nine Yards

The main question is, Can someone request to die rather than remain alive with a limb cut off?

[a] If Judaism believed that a person's life belongs to him or her, then he or she could decide whether to end it, and if life were worth living without a leg or another limb. However, the Jewish approach to life is that it belongs, along with our bodies, to God. A person is not the ultimate judge of his or her existence. It is for this reason that suicide is a sin in Judaism. Furthermore, all life has infinite value (*Sanhedrin* 37a), whether it is a life with one leg or two.

[b] From the surgeon's perspective, there is also no choice. He is commanded to help someone in danger by the Torah, which states, "DO NOT STAND IDLY BY THE BLOOD OF YOUR NEIGHBOR." (Leviticus 19:16). This means that one has a positive obligation to rescue someone in danger. (*Shulḥan Arukh* 426:1).

[c] Normally, it is forbidden to injure a person by cutting off a limb (Maimonides, *Hilkhot Hovel u'Mazik* 5:1) since this causes damage to the body, which belongs to God. But such an act performed in order to save a life is not only permitted, but is obligatory. Even if the victim objects to severing a limb, the obligation to save a person's life is not conditional on his or her consent.

Therefore, the surgeon is obligated to amputate the leg, and the injured person is obligated to allow him to do so if this action will save the victim's life.

[41] Keeping Peace in the Family

Ever since she was a little girl, Rhonda strongly believed in the concept of peace—not only between nations, but between individual people as well. She could never stand it when her parents argued. Then one day, she noticed that her younger sister Joy was taking her favorite clothes. Joy had never been the same size as Rhonda; but now that she was, things fit. Joy was wearing Rhonda's clothes to school, to dances and elsewhere, and she had never asked her sister. Rhonda knew that if she mentioned anything to Joy, it would start a fight. Being the peace-lover that she was, Rhonda avoided starting a fight, even though she knew that Joy was in the wrong. But in order to get her clothes back, there would have to be a big confrontation.

YOU BE THE JUDGE: *What should Rhonda do?*

The Answer to Keeping Peace in the Family

Is it proper to give up on an important idea, position or possession in order to keep peace and avoid confrontation? The question is applicable to physical things and in conversations that we have. What do Jewish sources say about how far must we go to avoid confrontation, or do they say so at all?

[a] The concept of establishing and maintaining peace is one of the most fundamental ideas in Judaism. One of the three pillars upon which the world is built is peace (*Pirke Avot* 1:18). Peace is as important as all of God's creations (Midrash *Bamidbar Rabbah* 11:7), and it is said that "God makes peace and creates everything" (morning service, *Yotzer Or*). Peace is the only mitzvah after which one is commanded to run, as it says, "Seek peace and pursue it" (Psalms 34:15).

[b] What happens when the concept of peace comes into conflict with other important Jewish values seeming to call for conflict or confrontation? Even then, Judaism seems to call for peace. Although truth is another of the three pillars upon which the world is built, it is generally more important to keep peace than to keep truth. Even God "lied" in order to keep the peace between Abraham and Sarah (Midrash *Bamidbar Rabbah* 11:7). The same midrash states that even if the Jews were to worship idols, they would not be severely punished if they were at peace with each other. This can be proven by the Torah story in which the builders of the Tower of Babel rebel against God (Genesis 11) but are not punished with death, since they are united (Genesis 11:1). On the other hand, Noah's generation is wiped out because of violence and conflict among people.

Therefore, it seems that a person is obligated to give up almost everything in order to achieve peace. This is true in a family, in a town, or in the entire Jewish nation. Of course, if "giving in" for the sake of peace will only lead to further conflict (because the other party sees that you are always giving in) then it should not be done, since it will not lead to peace. That is the reason that the Torah allows war. If the Jews were known for always giving in, their enemies would continually conquer and destroy them. In addition, there are always the "exceptions" for which one never gives up anything in Judaism. These include the sins of murder, sexual impropriety, and idol worship. However, peace supersedes almost everything else. Therefore, if it will achieve real peace with Joy, Rhonda should "give up" her clothes.

[42] Cinema Veríte

All the 13-year-old girls in the class are going to the movies together on Sunday, and they plan to say that they are 11 years old in order to receive the cheaper children's rate. Jill knows that this is wrong and does not want to lie, but if she does not go along with this idea, she knows that her friends will shun her and she will not be "in" with the group.

YOU BE THE JUDGE: *Should Jill lie to fit in or not?*

The Answer to Cinema Verite

Should a person give in to peer pressure and do something that he or she knows is wrong? What if it is in order to maintain a friendship?

[a] We know that we *should* always do what is right. The Torah tells us what is proper (mitzvot) and that we are supposed to imitate God's good ways (Deuteronomy 13:5) "...YOU SHOULD SERVE THE ETERNAL AND CLING TO GOD." Specifically, we are prohibited from lying (Leviticus 19: 11). It is the only sin in the Torah from which we are specifically commanded to run away: "...KEEP FAR FROM A LIE" (Exodus 23: 7).

[b] But Judaism also understands and is sensitive to the powerful pull of peer pressure from one's friends. For example, in the Korah rebellion, 250 people from the Tribe of Reuven team-up with Korah, who is from the Tribe of Levi (Numbers 16:1-2) to rebel against Moses. Rashi (commentary on Numbers 16:1) explains how the Reuvenites linked up with Korah: they were camped right next door. Ultimately, it was Korah's peer pressure that brought the 250 neighbors into the rebellion.

[c] In a similar fashion, when Lot's shepherds fought with Abraham's, the patriarch ordered both Lot and his herders to leave (Genesis 13:7-9). One explanation of why Abraham took such drastic action is that he was worried about the peer pressure that Lot's shepherds would push on his own men. Abraham understood that human beings are strongly influenced by the people with whom they spend time. Abraham chose to distance himself and his followers from the negative influence of Lot's helpers.

[d] In perhaps the most explicit Jewish acknowledgment of the power of peer pressure, Maimonides (*Hilkhot Deot* 6:1) agrees with Abraham that peer pressure is nearly impossible to overcome. He states that "It is in the very nature of people to be influenced by their peers, both in the way they think and the way they act." Therefore, rather than fight peer pressure, Maimonides tells us to make sure to spend time with good people who will pressure us to behave better, not worse, than our natural inclinations. In fact, Maimonides continues and says that if one cannot find good people to hang around, one should leave his/her city or even his/her country. If you cannot afford it, choose to live alone in the mountains rather than continue surrounding yourself with people who will negatively affect you. Thus, according to Maimonides, there is no effective way to combat the pull of peer pressure.

110

[e] Returning to our question, there are two parts to the answer. First, Jill should not lie. Secondly, we are aware of the dangers of peer pressure from people who do not push us to be better than our natural inclination, so it seems that Jill should try not to hang out with this group of friends. It is not worth maintaining friendships with people who lead you down dishonest and unholy paths.

[43] Is Ugliness in the Eye of the Beholder?

Each day, on their way to school, Danny and his friends pass a truly ugly, deformed man, who sits on the street and sells pens and pencils. He has a deformed face, one deformed arm and no legs. Danny is really "turned off" by the sight of this man, and always looks away in order not to stare at this deformed person. However, Danny's friends say that Danny should not react to the ugliness in this manner, and *should* look at the man in order not to embarrass him.

YOU BE THE JUDGE: *How should Danny and his friends view this person? Should they look or not look? Should they understand the man's deformity as a punishment from God?*

The Answer to Is Ugliness in the Eye of the Beholder?

How should a person react to physical ugliness and to differences between people? Surely these are personal kinds of determinations, but there is a part in each of us that sees some things as beautiful and some things as ugly. Does it make a difference if one of those "things" is another human being? Check the sources:

[a] It is natural to react to anyone who is different, and sometimes we are jolted by people who are deformed. The rabbis understood this natural reaction, and the *Shulhan Arukh* codified a proper Jewish reaction based on the Talmud (*Berakhot* 58a). Rabbi Joseph Karo writes (*Shulhan Arukh, Orekh Hayyim* 225:9) that upon seeing a deformed person, including someone who is extremely pockmarked or missing a limb, a Jew is supposed to recite the blessing "Blessed is the God who makes different types of creations." The reasoning behind such a blessing is the acknowledgment that all creatures, no matter how repulsive or how different, are still God's creations.

[b] How *does* Judaism view ugliness and deformity? While requiring everyone to be treated equally, Judaism certainly does not prefer deformity. For example, a deformed person cannot serve as a priest in the Jewish Temple (Leviticus 21:17). In addition, there is a difference between a person who was born deformed and one who became deformed in an accident. In the latter case, the *Shulhan Arukh* (228:9) prescribes the following blessing: "Blessed is Adonai, who is the True Judge," It is the same blessing one recites upon hearing of the death of a relative, to indicate that we cannot understand why God does certain things in the world. When it comes to ugliness, Judaism seems to look at physical beauty as something positive, whether it be in people (*Megillah* 15a), animals (Jerusalem Talmud, *Avodah Zarah* 8a) or places (*Esther Rabbah* 1:16). And we know that most people prefer not to be ugly. However, one man, Rabbi Joshua, the ugliest man in the Talmud, actually preferred to be ugly. He said (*Taanit* 7a) that he could not have become such a great scholar had he been physically attractive, implying that the time he would have needed to devote to maintaining physical attractiveness would have taken away from his studies.

[d] While the *Shulhan Arukh* rules that we make a blessing in reaction to being repulsed, its writer adds a crucial addendum (225:8): We should only make a blessing the first time we see an ugly, deformed person. After that, the blessing is not recited. Why is this so? It is clear that after the first time, the ugliness and repulsion are never felt as strongly. With God's help, we begin to see past the exterior of a person and examine his or her personality. With this, the ugliness naturally fades. We begin to define the person by inner, and not outer, qualities. Even if we never get to know the person, the blessing helps center us in terms of how we should look at the human being in front of us. This is why, when watching films about ugly people or things, we are not as shocked by the ugliness after a while.

Returning to our original question, it is proper to react to the man's deformity, and even to recite a blessing, but only the first time. After the effort has been made to get to know the person and recognize that God created him, just as the Eternal created other human beings, the repulsion should fade.

[44] Who's Kidding Who?

Sam and Judy Marcus are very successful in their separate careers. They nonetheless manage to find some quality time to spend with each other during their busy weeks to continue improving their marriage (there is always room for improvement; it's part of loving and growing). Although money is certainly not an issue, they decide that it would be better not to bring any children into the world because a) they would not be able to devote adequate time to a child due to their careers; b) the child would hold back their careers; and, c) the world is so full of hate and anger that any way you look at it, it would be unfair to bring an innocent child into it.

YOU BE THE JUDGE: *Is there any validity to such a decision not to have children?*

The Answer to Who's Kidding Who?

Is it legitimate to decide not to have children for personal reasons?

[a] The importance of having children in Judaism cannot be overemphasized. The Talmud states (*Nedarim* 64b) that a person who does not have children is considered to be dead.

[b] Is there any justification for not having children? If the reason for not having children is economic—i.e. there is not enough money to feed the family or not enough food in the world for all the people—then there is precedent for not having or delaying having children. We learn this from looking closely at the story of Joseph, who had his children before, but not during, the famine in Egypt (Genesis 41:50). Based on Joseph's intentional act of family planning, the Talmud (*Ta'anit* 11a) says that in times of famine, when food is unavailable, one should not have children.

[c] In codifying this law, Maimonides (*Hilkhot Ta'anit* 3:8) states that the law of not having children during a famine applies only if you have already performed the mitzvah of having two children. Otherwise, the mitzvah of having children overrides any technicality that would allow people to remain childless. In the specific case above, careers and issues about evil in the world, are not valid reasons to ignore the mitzvah to "BE FRUITFUL AND MULTIPLY."

Let us remember that this entire concept is based on the notion that weather conditions can create a food shortage and children would suffer because of it. We know from many studies (see *NY Times*, December 7, 1981) that ample food is produced each year to feed every single human on the planet. The only reason that famine exists (more than 40,000 people die each DAY from famine) is the economic/political problem of distributing the vast food stores to the poorest countries (tons of grain is burned each year in order to keep prices down and stable).

[45] A Clean War

When his parents were discussing how much Judaism opposes the killing of human beings, especially the killing of innocent people, Elliot asked them: "If that is so, then how can Judaism ever allow any war to take place since that involves killing people?" Try as they may, Elliot's parents could not give Elliot a satisfying answer to his question.

YOU BE THE JUDGE: *Is there an answer to Elliot's question?*

The Answer to A Clean War

Does Judaism allow any type of war or only specific types? If Jews are opposed to killing, how can Judaism ever allow for war?

[a] It is true that killing another human being is one of the most serious sins in the Torah. If it will help him stay alive, a Jew is required to commit every sin in the Torah—except for murder, sexual impropriety, and idol worship (*Sanhedrin* 74a). Jewish law did allow for the death penalty, but a court was called "bloody" if it put more than one person to death every 70 years (*Makkot* 7a)! So how does Judaism allow war, since killing is such an integral part of it?

[b] The Torah recognizes that sometimes war is a necessary evil, even though people may be killed. If the Torah totally opposed war, the nations of the world might take advantage of the "pacifist" Jews. Nations might feel free to attack, capture, subjugate and/or kill Jews, use their land and natural resources at will, thus depriving the Jewish people of their lifestyle, their values, and their freedom to worship God. In order to prevent such a situation from occurring (both on an individual basis as well as nationally), the Torah allows individuals to kill in self-defense when their lives are threatened (Exodus 22:1). In addition, the Torah provides for a Jewish army in order to maintain the Jewish people's independence and way of life (Deuteronomy 22). Even the most traditionally "pacifist" country, Switzerland, maintains a standing army for the same reasons. However, we will see that a Jewish war comes only as a last resort, and with many conditions.

[c] From the story of the very first Jew, we can see the establishment of the pattern of the Jewish attitude of war. Abraham was a peace-loving man who invited every stranger to dine with him in his tent (*Sotah* 10b). Yet when it was absolutely necessary, this man of peace resorted to battle. When his nephew Lot was captured by the enemy in the midst of a thirteen-year world war, Abraham and his men immediately defeated the four kings who were their enemies and ended the war in order to free Lot. However, they refused to take any spoils (Genesis 14:14-24). Thus, Abraham never sought war, but when forced to fight, he did so and was victorious.

[d] In Jewish law, only three types of wars are permitted (Maimonides, *Hilkhot Melakhim* 5:1). One war is to fight and destroy the nation of Amalek, whose avowed purpose is to destroy all Jews and

118

Judaism. The second is to destroy the Seven Nations who lived in the Land of Israel and represented a lifestyle antithetical to Judaism (these nations no longer exist today). The third is a war for self-defense. Wars for other purposes are forbidden, except under special circumstances. Even when fighting a "legitimate" war, actual battle and killing are considered a last resort. (Maimonides, *Hilkhot Melakhim* 6:7).

[46] Civil Disobedience

Martin Luther King Jr. became famous when he intentionally broke certain laws in a non-violent way. He used the method of sitting down in the middle of a street and being arrested in protest. He was calling attention to the lack of civil rights in America and to Jim Crow laws that discriminated against blacks in the South. This was known as civil disobedience. Was Martin Luther King Jr. right to knowingly break the law?

YOU BE THE JUDGE: *Is it ever right to break a country's laws, even in protest? Is it ever right to break a Jewish law for the same reason?*

The Answer to Civil Disobedience

Is it ever right to refuse to obey the law as an act of civil disobedience? Can you break a law to achieve a higher ideal?

[a] There are numerous examples in the Bible where individuals were civilly disobedient and seem to be praised for their actions. The midwives in Egypt refused to listen to Pharaoh's decree to kill Jewish babies because they feared God (Exodus 1:15-19). When King Saul ordered his guards to kill the Jewish priests in the city of Nov, they refused (I Samuel 22:16-17). When the prophet Daniel was forbidden to pray, he ignored that order by the king and prayed anyway, which is why he was thrown into the famous lion's den (Daniel 6:7-14).

[b] The Torah itself seems to anticipate the "classic" act of civil disobedience, protesting a war, by allowing a soldier to return home if he is "weak of heart" (Deuteronomy 20:5-8). According to some commentaries on the Mishnah (*Sotah* 8:5-6), this refers to a "conscientious objector," someone who objects to the idea of war itself. His protest is allowed, and he is not forced to fight. These examples seem to clearly point to a Jewish acceptance, or even requirement, of opposition toward immoral or improper government decisions.

[c] However, there is an opposing Jewish principle called *Dina D'Malkhuta Dina*, which applies especially outside the land of Israel. It means "The law of the land is the law," and it maintains that Jews must follow the local government and its edicts. This insures a strong central authority, which inevitably protects Jews. It is for this reason that the Mishnah (*Pirke Avot* 3:6) says that Jews should pray for the welfare of their government. Thus, it seems that while a Jew may, on occasion, be civilly disobedient, he or she may not disobey the laws of any legitimate government to the point that may endanger that regime. Of course, if the government is ruthless or immoral, or enacts anti-Torah laws, then certainly civil disobedience could be considered as a way to protest.

[d] Maimonides (*Hilkhot Melakhim* 3:9) says that a Jew must refuse to obey even a king who forbids following the Torah.

[47] A Man in Need of Aid

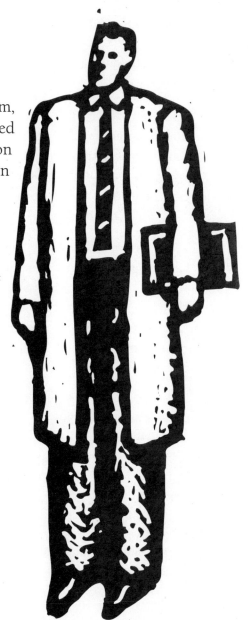

a patient with AIDS is brought into the emergency room, and needs an immediate operation on his infected spleen, or he will die within twenty-four hours. But the surgeon on call refuses to operate because he refuses to put himself in mortal danger for someone who will die shortly anyway.

YOU BE THE JUDGE: *Is this doctor required to treat this AIDS patient?*

The Answer to A Man in Need of Aid

Is a doctor permitted to refuse to operate on an AIDS patient based on the patient's short life expectancy and the potential risk to the doctor's own life?

[a] There is certainly a mitzvah to save someone who is in danger of losing his or her life. The Torah says, "YOU SHALL NOT STAND IDLY BY WHILE YOUR FELLOW'S BLOOD IS BEING SPILLED" (Leviticus 19:16). The *Shulḥan Arukh* (*Yoreh Deah* 336:1) applies this obligation specifically to doctors who can save a sick patient. However, we must ask ourselves if this verse and this law have different applications when there is a risk to the doctor.

[b] The Talmudic discussion about the obligation to save someone's life makes no specific mention of the impending risks or danger to the saver. However, the *Mishnah Berurah*, a Twentieth Century commentary on Jewish law, clearly states (*Orekh Ḥayyim* 329:8:19) that one must not put oneself at risk, or even possible risk, in order to save someone in mortal danger.

[c] The *Beit Yosef* commentary (Sixteenth Century) on the *Tur* (*Ḥoshen Mishpat* 626) disagrees. In it, Rabbi Joseph Karo explains that the logic behind the general ruling to save a dying person is that while the "saver" is only in possible danger, the person being saved is in definite danger, and thus takes precedence. Thus, we see that according to this opinion, a person must indeed put him or herself at risk to save a dying person. However, the final *halakhah* (Jewish law ruling, literally "way to go") sides with the *Mishnah Berurah*, agreeing that a person may not put him or herself in grave danger to save someone else.

[d] The Jewish definition of risk is discussed in several Responsa (notably *Radbaz*, quoted by Rav Moshe Feinstein, Responsa *Yoreh Deah*, Section II:174:4). Based on many sources, they conclude that if the risk is truly great (1 in 10, according to Rav Herschel Schecter of Yeshiva University), then it would be forbidden to save someone, even if you wanted to do so. If the risk to the "saver" is less (one in 100), then a person is permitted to save under such a risk, but is not obligated to. However, if the risk is truly minimal (less than 1 in 1000), then this is not even considered risk in Jewish law, and one would be obligated to save a person who is dying.

Returning to our original question, we can now answer clearly based on the odds and risk. Since we know that hundreds of thousands of successful operations have been performed on AIDS patients over the years, and only one or two doctors and nurses have contracted the disease as a result, then the risk to the doctor is certainly less than one in 1000. The doctor is therefore obligated to perform the operation to save the life of the AIDS patient.